D1741878

WELFARE RIGHTS

Welfare Rights

A Bibliography on Law and the Poor
1970-1975

Martin Partington
John Hull
Susan Knight

 Frances Pinter

First Published in Great Britain in 1976 by
Frances Pinter (Publishers) Limited
161 West End Lane, London, NW6 2LG

Printed in Great Britain by
Billing and Sons Limited
Guildford, Surrey

ISBN 0 903804 15 8   paperback
ISBN 0 903804 16 6   hardback

INTRODUCTION

Unlike the situation in the U.S.A. or Canada, bibliographies on British law and law-related subjects are rare in Britain. To find out what the relevant literature is on any given subject-area is, therefore, always a lengthy and complex process, especially with a topic that is itself newly-developing. Thus the general objective of this bibliography is to help fill one of the many gaps which currently exist.

At this point, one problematic question must be raised which goes to the issue of whether this book should have been prepared at all. Many people welcome the development of welfare rights as a highly desirable, even praiseworthy, activity in which lawyers, social workers and others, should have been involved long ago, and which may lead them to make a fundamental contribution to the wider objective of the elimination of basic inequalities in our society. Others, however, are much more sceptical. They see the development of interest as just another way for lawyers, social workers, etc., to make money, and to develop professional reputations. It is argued that the long-term result of this will simply be to prop up a basically unsound system and postpone the day of radical change in society.

The compilers of this bibliography attempted to reach a compromise between these two positions. We concluded that the latter argument above, even if correct, need not result in our refusing to produce the bibliography at all. Rather we have attempted, particularly in the book section, to refer to material that does relate to the fundamental issues which underlie any concern with welfare rights. This process is assisted by the two bibliographies which have already been published in this series by Frances Pinter (Publishers) limited: Westergaard, et al, MODERN BRITISH SOCIETY (1974); and Blackstone, SOCIAL POLICY AND ADMINISTRATION IN BRITAIN (1975). They are intended to be used in conjunction with this volume, and frequent cross-references to those books are contained herein.

The idea of compiling this bibliography originated during the establishment of a legal advice service in Coventry in 1971. It seemed that at least four groups of people might obviously find such a reference work useful: first, practising lawyers who are employed in law centres or who run the (rather few) private legal offices which specialize in legal aid/welfare work; second, social workers, welfare rights, housing aid, consumer rights and community workers; third, the people involved in grass roots organizations, those who work for pressure groups, politicians and so forth who are campaigning for change or reform; fourth, both teachers and students of law, social administration, politics, economics, sociology, who are interested in the operation of the British welfare state. We felt that all these groups, due either to overwork, or to lack of familiarity with the field, could benefit from a guide to the relevant legal literature. We wished to sweep away some of the mystery that tends to surround the legal system and its workings, to the detriment of everyone (except professional lawyers), and to assist those involved in innovative work in the fields covered in this book.

Setting limits to the scope of the book was more problematic. "Welfare Rights" has no fixed parameters. The easiest way to find out about what this book contains is to look at the Contents pages. What follows here are some observations of how we defined those contents:

(i) In general, we refer to material relevant to the development of the law which relates to the financially disadvantaged--either individuals or whole sections of the community--in our society. We were assisted in this by knowledge of the range of cases that typically come into neighbourhood law centres, advice centres, housing aid centres and so on. Thus we have included references to community issues such as planning, slum clearance and compulsory purchase as well as individual matters, such as social security.

However, a number of arbitrary bounds were set which inevitably derive from our perceptions of what problems low-income groups face, which may not correspond with the issues they perceive as important. (Suggestions for altering the scope of the work for any possible future editions will, of course, be welcomed.) For example, there are no references to those topics conventionally classified as "Civil Liberties" (e.g. police powers, immigration or racial and sexual discrimination). Labour law topics are, for the most part, ignored. (Though see, Hepple, Nelson and O'Higgins: BIBLIOGRAPHY OF BRITISH AND IRISH LABOUR LAW, Mansell, 1975). And only selected family law issues are included.

(ii) For Section A of the bibliography, we only examined British legal periodicals. Although there is a vast amount of relevant writing in other sources such as NEW SOCIETY, and in social work, community work, sociology and economics journals, we wanted in particular to make legal materials more accessible. Further, we wanted to produce the book relatively speedily and to have gone further afield would have caused considerable delay in completing the work. Additionally it would have made it much more expensive to produce.

10

From the periodicals listed, we have included references to a vast variety of material, ranging from long analytical articles to much shorter descriptive or editorial pieces. The major limitation here is that we have only gone back as far as 1970, on the assumption that it was only from around that time that substantial amounts of relevant material came to be written. A feature of this section of this bibliography is that brief notes of the contents of the majority of the articles which are referred to are given.

(iii)   For Section B, the range of books concentrates on British material. In a broad sense, the contents of this section mirror the topics which are contained in Section A. But it was not possible to achieve a direct correlation between the two sections. In particular, as already noted, we wanted to refer to material which raised more fundamental issues about the role of law in the welfare rights area. Therefore, the material cited in this section is not exclusively legal in character. Furthermore, the opportunity was taken to extend the scope of the work by referring to a fair amount of relevant American and Commonwealth literature.

ACKNOWLEDGMENTS

Many people have helped in the production of this bibliography. At the London School of Economics, Susan Kirk laboured with her usual excellence at transferring illegible index cards into typed copy. Thanks should also be extended to the administrators of the L.S.E.'s legal research division for their financial support. At Osgoode Hall Law School, York University, Toronto, Professor Balfour Halevy was of great assistance in the Library. The typesetting itself was done on the I.B.M. Composer of the law students' Legal and Lit. Society. Our thanks must be extended to the officers of the Society and to Betty Laverty for all their help in arranging this. The type itself was expertly set by Barby Wolfish. Daphne Scharen kindly assisted with checking proofs.

Toronto and London   Martin Partington
April, 1976   John Hull
                                                       Susan Knight

12

List of Journals Consulted and Citations

British Journal of Law and Society	B.J.L.A.S.
British Tax Review	B.T.R.
Cambridge Law Journal	C.L.J.
Community Action	COMMUNITY ACTION
Conveyancer & Property Lawyer	CONVEYANCER
Criminal Law Review	CRIM. L.R.
Family Law	FAMILY LAW
Industrial Law Journal	I.L.J.
International & Comparative Law Quarterly	I.C.L.Q.
Journal of Planning Law (until 1972)	J.P.L.
Journal of Planning Law & Environment Law (from 1973)	J.P.E.L.
Journal of the Society of Public Teachers of Law	J.S.P.T.L.
Law Guardian (appears as Guardian/Gazette after 1973)	LAW GUARDIAN
Law Notes	LAW NOTES
Law Quaterly Review	L.Q.R.
Law Society Gazette	L.S.GAZ.
Law Teacher	LAW TEACHER
Legal Action Group Bulletin	LAG.BULL.
Local Government Review (from 1972)	L.G.R.
Juridicial Review	JUR.REV.
Justice of the Peace (from 1972)	J.P.
Justice of the Peace and Local Government Review (until 1971)	J.P. & L.G.R.
Modern Law Review	M.L.R.
New Law Journal	N.L.J.
Northern Ireland Legal Quarterly	N.I.L.Q.
Poverty	POVERTY
Public Law	PUB.L.
Roof	ROOF
Solicitor's Journal	S.J.

OTHER ABBREVIATIONS

ALL E.R.	All England Law Reports
B.L.A.	British Legal Association
C.P.A.G.	Child Poverty Action Group
C.A.B.x	Citizens' Advice Bureaux
Cd., Cmd., Cmnd.	Command Papers
C.P.O.	Compulsory Purchase Order
C.A.	Court of Appeal
Cr.App.R.	Criminal Appeal Reports
DoE	Department of the Environment
D.H.S.S.	Department of Health and Social Security
ex p.	ex parte
F.I.S.	Family Income Supplement
G.M.A.	Guaranteed Maintenance Allowance
H.M.S.O.	Her Majesty's Stationery Office
H.L.	House of Lords
L.G.	Local Government
L.C.O.	Lord Chancellor's Office
N.C.C.L.	National Council for Civil Liberties
N.I.	National Insurance
N.L.C.	Neighbourhood Law Centre
P.C.A.	Parliamentary Commissioner for Administration
S.	Section
S.I.	Statutory Instrument
S.B.	Supplementary Benefits
S.B.A.T.	Supplementary Benefits Appeal Tribunal
S.B.C.	Supplementary Benefits Commission
W.L.R.	Weekly Law Reports

SECTION A

PERIODICAL LITERATURE

1970-1975

(See also   Westergaard, pp 32-4, 110-2; and Blackstone, pp 38, 96-7)

(a)   LEGAL ADVICE AND ASSISTANCE

1970

Anon. LAW GUARDIAN No. 55 p. 4   'Practical Legal Aid'   Comment on
Lord Chancellor's Advisory Committee's acceptance of the 25-pound
scheme proposal
—   67 L.S.GAZ 82   'Report on the Lord Chancellor's Committee on Legal
Advice and Assistance'   Short editorial article on nature and case for
the 25-pound scheme
—   120 N.L.J. 25   'Legal Advice and Assistance'   Review of Cmnd. 4249
'The Better Provision of Legal Advice and Assistance' by Lord
Chancellor's Advisory Committee. Also see p. 26 'Help for the Legal
Needy — The Future'   A continuation of the above review
—   120 N.L.J. 1054   'The 25-pound scheme — A Question of Priority'
Editorial
—   PUBLIC LAW 197   'Legal Advice'   Comment on details of Cmnd.
4249 (Report of Lord Chancellor's Advisory Committee on Legal
Advice and Assistance)
114 S.J. 41   'Legal Advice'   Comment on 25-pound scheme, and
advisory liason officer scheme
Brooke, R. 33 M.L.R. 432   'Report of the Advisory Committee on Legal Advice
and Assistance'

1971

Anon. LAW GUARDIAN No. 75 p. 2   'The 25-pound scheme'   Short
note on 25-pound scheme
—   68 L.S.GAZ 300   'The 20th Annual Report of the Law Society with the
Lord Chancellor's Advisory Committee's Comments: It Would Be a
Tragic Mistake. . . '   Comment on the 20th Report, in particular on
its emphasis that the 25-pound scheme must be implemented soon
—   115 S.J. 533   'Pressing the 25-pound Scheme'   Note on Lord
Chancellor's Advisory Committee's desire to press on with scheme

Anon. 136 J.P. 123 'Legal Advice and Assistance' Comment on Legal
Advice and Assistance Bill

— LAW GUARDIAN No. 78 p. 3 (a) 'Legal Aid – And By Whom?'
and (b) 'The Shape of Things to Come' Editorial notes (a) on Legal
Advice and Assistance Bill; and (b) on Legal Aid and Advice (Local
Legal Centres) Bill presented by Michael Meacher, M.P.

— 69 L.S.GAZ No. 9, p. 1 'Legal Advice and Criminal Appeals –
A Survey of Prisoners, Prisons and Lawyers' – by M. Zander (1972
Crim. L.R. 132) Editorial Comment

— LAG BULL. No. 6, p. 2 'Legal Advice and Assistance – Where
are We Now?' LAG's reaction to Attorney-General's Commons'
announcement that Part II 1972 Act would not be implemented
until 25-pound scheme showed its effectiveness. Editorial comment
that setting up of liaison scheme is matter of urgency

— 122 N.L.J. 117 'Statutory Legal Assistance' Note on introduction
of Legal Advice and Assistance Bill – 25-pound scheme

— 122 N.L.J. 231 'Legal Assistance – Striding on the Spot'
Editorial reviewing North Kensington Law Centre's criticism of the
Legal Advice and Assistance Bill

— 122 N.L.J. 384 'More Advice. More Assistance' Summary of
critical statements on the Legal Advice and Assistance Bill, made
by (a) CPAG, and (b) NCCL

— 122 N.L.J. 526 'Legal Advice – The Shifting Scene' Editorial
on 25-pound scheme, and its passage from the Commons to the
Lords; a look at the scheme now, in relation to alternative sources
of legal aid and advice

— 116 S.J. 109 '25-pound scheme on the Way' Note on Legal Advice
and Assistance Bill

— 116 S.J. 421 'The Right to See A Solicitor' Comment on M.
Zander's article in (1972) Crim. L.R. 342 where he suggests that
police prevent suspects obtaining access to legal advice (and see LEGAL
SERVICES, 1972)

Hodge, H. 23 POVERTY 21 'The Legal Advice & Assistance Bill'
Summary of CPAG memorandum to MPs on the Committee stage of
this Bill

Pollock, S. 69 L.S.GAZ No. 16, p. 365 'Legal Advice and Assistance –
Does The Bill Go Far Enough?' The article deals in general terms
with the Legal Advice and Assistance Bill, and in particular with
tribunals, coroner's courts and small claims

Pollock, S. 122 N.L.J. 807 'Legal Advice and Assistance Act 1972 – The Scheme and a Mis-appraisal' Criticism of account given by A. Samuels of this new Act at (1972) N.L.J. 696

Samuels, A. 35 M.L.R. 630 'Legal Advice and Assistance Act 1972' Short review of Act; contains good bibliography of materials on Act and general area

– 122 N.L.J. 696 'Legal Advice and Assistance Act 1972 – The Scheme and an Appraisal'

Sanctuary, G. 69 L.S.GAZ 902 'Advertising Legal Aid – The Tyne-Tees Campaign'

Zander, M. CRIM.L.R. 132 'Legal Advice and Criminal Appeals: A survey of Prisoners, Prisons and Lawyers' Report of survey, with notes on methodology and a whole range of statistics and views. The whole issue is devoted to this one article; editorial at p. 129 explains why (See also, LEGAL SERVICES, 1972)

– 69 L.S.GAZ 874 'Pro Bono Publico' A substantial note on the Legal Advice and Assistance Act, 1972

1973

Anon. 22 I.C.L.Q. 581 'Legal Aid: Great Britain' Legal Advice and Assistance Act 1972 – short run-down on the Act and 25-pound scheme

– J.P.E.L. 342 'Part I Legal Aid and Assistance Act 1972: The 25-pound Scheme'

– 137 J.P. 98 'Developments in Legal Aid' Note on Lord Chancellor's Advisory Committee's views that income and capital levels should be revised upwards before Part I Legal Advice & Assistance Act, 1972, comes into operation

– 137 J.P. 196 'Legal Advice and Assistance' Note on introduction of Parts I and III of Legal Advice and Assistance Act, 1972

– 137 J.P. 402 'Advice and Assistance' Note on Lord Chancellor's Advisory Committee's 22nd Report

– 137 J.P. 674 'Natural Justice and the Social Worker' Comment on extent to which accused person can be advised or represented by non-lawyers

– 70 L.S.GAZ 1562 'Council Statement – Voluntary Legal Advice Scheme' On implementation of Parts I and III Legal Advice and Assistance Act 1972, voluntary legal advice scheme will cease

– LAG BULL. 26 'A Soft Sell' The 25-scheme. LAG criticizes the Law Society's failure to explain to solicitors the nature of the work that deprived areas can offer to them. LAG's attitude is that an opportunity to explain this has been missed

Anon. LAG BULL. 83 'Advice and Assistance On the Application of English Law' Editorial on Legal Advice and Assistance Act 1972 and way in which it extends possibilities of solicitors' work into previously unprofitable and often uncharted areas of law and ways in which profession should be equipped to deal with increasing work load; followed by chart showing these areas and their potentialities for legal practitioners

− LAG BULL. 148 'Family Income Supplement and New Legal Aid' Note on effect of Family Income Supplement on Legal Aid Scheme

− 117 S.J. 233, 243 'New Legal Advice and Assistance Scheme' Lord Chancellor's press release describing the 25-pound scheme

Hillyard, S. LAG BULL. 44 'The New Legal Advice and Assistance Scheme' Analysis of the new scheme

Pollock, S. 70 L.S.GAZ. 1508 'Legal Advice and Assistance; The New Deal' The article (a) deals with practitioners and the public, (b) deals with how local Law Societies can play an integral part in this scheme, e.g. duty solicitors, advice centres and liaison with CABx

− 117 S.J. 176 'Legal Aid: The New Advice Scheme' Full statement on new scheme

Sanctuary, G. 70 L.S.GAZ 2272 'Advertising the Legal Aid Scheme'

1974

Anon. 138 J.P. 174 'Legal Advice and Assistance' Comment on recommendations to new Lord Chancellor by Advisory Committee on Legal Aid and Advice in report of 1972-73

− 71 L.S.GAZ 135 'Practice Note: The New Advice Scheme' National Insurance Commissioner's advice on the new legal advice scheme

− LAG BULL. 234 'Has the Green Form Scheme Worked?' Abridged version of a study of LAG's solicitor members on working of Green Form scheme

Glasser, C. 3 I.L.J. 62 'Social Security – Legal Aid and Advice Act 1972'
A review of Act. Also special sections on 'Trade Unions and Legal
Advice', 'Tribunals', 'Salaried Solicitors'

Harper, T. 124 N.L.J. 67 'LAG Survey into 'Green Form' Legal Aid
Scheme Workings' Note of survey about to be initiated by LAG to
discover how well the 25-pound Green Form Legal Assistance scheme
is working

Pollock, S. 71 L.S.GAZ 123 'The Green Form Scheme – How is it Going?'
Report of C.O.I. commissioned survey of first five months of 25-pound
scheme

Smith, P. 124 N.L.J. 750 'Welfare Law in Practice' Article on recognition
by legal profession of problems encountered in area of poverty law,
and nature of area they will have to familiarise themselves with, as the
25-pound scheme grows

1975

Adamsdown Community & Advice Centre. LAG BULL. 35 'In praise of
the Green Form – sort of' Use of the Green Form Scheme to finance
an independent report for use by residents in opposing a council's
redevelopment scheme

Anon. LAG BULL. 41 'Advocacy under the Green Form Scheme' Survey
of possible situations where solicitor can act as advocate under Legal
Aid Act 1974 s. 2(4)

(b)   LEGAL AID (EXCLUDING CRIMINAL LEGAL AID)

1970

Anon. 134 J.P. & L.G.R. 2 'Legal Aid: Successful Defendants' Costs'
Editorial on failure, until Hanning v. Maitland, of Legal Aid Act
1964 to assist successful, but unassisted, defendants; explanation
of case law in area

–   LAW GUARDIAN No. 59 p. 5 'Legal Aid Changes Wanted' Short
note on Cobden Trust paper on Legal Aid scheme

–   LAW GUARDIAN No. 60 p. 1 'Legal Aid for Trustees' Note on
R. v. Legal Aid Committee No. 9 (1970) 1 All E.R. 1176, on trustees
applying for legal aid

–   67 L.S. GAZ 587 'The 19th Annual Report to the Lord Chancellor on
the Operation and Finance of the Legal Aid and Advice Scheme'

Anon. 120 N.L.J. 286 'Legal Aid as a Social Service' Review of Cobden Trust's 'Legal Aid as a Social Service'

— 120 N.L.J. 723 'Legal Aid – A case for Research' Need for research into legal aid – its working, cover, variations in the country,

— 120 N.L.J. 1051 'Making Justice Available to All' Report on Professor G. Borrie's Lecture 'Law Reform: A Damp Squib?'; emphasising that ordinary people should be able to enforce legal rights without bankrupting themselves

— 120 N.L.J. 1054 'Legal Aid – Contributions and Disregards' Comment on changes in disposable income limits

— 114 S.J. 14 'Hanning v. Maitland (C.A.)' Legal aid: successful unassisted defendant: whether entitled to costs from public funds; meaning of 'severe financial hardship'

— 114 S.J. 233 'Legal Aid' Comment on Cobden Trust report 'Legal Aid as a Social Service'

— 114 S.J. 577 'Legal Aid Year' Editorial comment on expansion and development of the legal aid and advice scheme, as borne out by statistics contained in Lord Chancellor's Committee's 19th Report 1968-69

Drewry, G. 120 N.L.J. 488 'Social Science and Legal Aid and Advice' Legal aid – a field calling for high degree of co-operation between sociologists and lawyers – possibilities of reform suggested in 'Legal Aid as a Social Service' by Cobden Trust (and see LAWYERS AND SOCIAL WORKERS)

F.G. 114 S.J. 403 'Legal Aid: Successful Defendant's Costs' A review of the award of costs in cases where an unrepresented litigant is successful, in light of Hanning v. Maitland (No. 2) (1970). Review of court's interpretations of what is meant by "Just and equitable" and "Severe financial hardship" in Legal Aid Act 1964

— 114 S.J. 817 'Representative Litigant and Legal Aid' Position of person suing in representative, offficial or fiduciary capacity examined

Pollock, S. 67 L.S.GAZ 399 'Legal Aid as a Social Service – The Cobden Trust Report' Concentrates principally on what the Report has to say about civil legal aid

Samuels, A. 120 N.L.J. 124 'The Local Secretary's Powers' Administration of local legal aid scheme and powers (and consequent drawbacks) of local secretary of legal aid committees

Waters, R.L. 114 S.J. 594 'Legal Aid: Children and Young Persons' s. 33 (read in conjunction with Schedules I and VI) of Children and Young Persons Act 1969 deals with grant of legal aid. This article considers how the section and schedules work

1971

Anon. 1 FAMILY LAW 161   'Divorce after two years'   separation – Legal Aid'

– 135 J.P. & L.G.R. 552   'Legal Aid Deficiency'   Suggests that defendants who are known or suspected to be mentally disordered should also be legally represented – deficiency of legal aid scheme on this problem

– 68 L.S.GAZ 241   'The Cobden Trust Report'   Editorial containing a report to criticisms of the Law Society by the Cobden Trust on the Law Society's approach and attitude towards legal aid schemes

– 121 N.L.J. 79   'Legal Aid Regulations'   Details

– 121 N.L.J. 677   'Legal Aid – A Cost Analysis'   Statistics and costing of legal aid scheme (editorial)

– 115 S.J. 22   'Legal Aid and Costs'   Comment on decision in Saunders v. Anglia Building Society on payment of respondent's costs from legal aid fund

Earnshaw, T.K. & Hand, J. 121 N.L.J. 492   'Successful Unassisted Party's Costs'   Construction of Legal Aid Act 1964, which was intended to alleviate financial hardship caused to unassisted litigant against his assisted opponent.   Cases on this Act reviewed

Gibson, C. 1 FAMILY LAW 90, 122   'The effect of Legal Aid on divorce in England and Wales – Part I: before 1950, Part II: since 1950'

Pollock, S. 115 S.J. 898   'Legal Aid: Giving Reasons'   Exploration of the reasons given in Legal Aid Committee decisions

Sufrin, B. & Bridges, L.T. 121 N.L.J. 869   'Statutory Legal Aid in Birmingham'   Results of research on this topic in Birmingham area – statistics

Waters, R.L. 115 S.J. 150   'The Legal Aid (General) Regulations 1971 (S.I. No. 62)'

– 115 S.J. 730   'Wife's Liability for Costs and Legal Aid'   Povey v. Povey (1971) 2 W.L.R. 381   highlights number of problems in connection with s.1 Legal Aid Act 1964, particularly with wife's liability in costs in matrimonial proceedings

1972

Anon. 136 J.P. 173   'Legal Aid'   Concentrates on wording of forms which leads to misunderstandings on means – test levels, result being that loss is caused to public funds since no contribution can be assessed on wrongly stated income levels; fault of difficult form, not applicants

– 136 J.P. 405   'Legal Aid and Advice'   Lord Chancellor's Advisory Committee Report 1970/71

Anon.   LAW GUARDIAN No. 80 p. 9   'Legal Aid and Advice'   Article
on Law Society conference on Legal Aid
–   LAG BULL. No. 4 p. 10   'Legal Aid: The Law Society Reports and
the Advisory Committee Comments'   Summary of 21st Annual Report
–   122 N.L.J. 647   'Just and Equitable?'   S. 1(2) Legal Aid Act 1964:
'Just and equitable' orders in considering whether costs can be paid
out of public funds: immaterial that successful opponent of legally-
aided litigant is wealthy insurance company – General Accident, Fire
& Life Ltd. v. Frew
–   116 S.J. 185   'Legal Aid Costs'   Note on Beales v. Beales – which
held that a respondent, however affluent, to a suit under s. 2(1)(d)
Divorce Reform Act 1969, could not, under any circumstances, be
compelled to pay costs. (See also: 'Costs of Consent Divorce' at
p. 189 and at p. 250 'Further Thoughts on Consent Divorce Costs')
–   116 S.J. 261   'Costs Payable by Legal Aid Fund'   Note on Clifford
v. Walker in which Court of Appeal held that all unassisted successful
litigants had to show a 'just and equitable' case to be paid costs
–   116 S.J. 473   'Legal Aid'   Comment on Lord Chancellor's Advisory
Committee's 21st report calling for upward revision of capital and
income limits
Denning, Lord 69 L.S.GAZ No. 2 p. 5   'Rt. Hon. Lord Denning M.R. . . . .
Legal Aid'
Greer, D. & Carson, D.   LAG BULL. No. 5 p. 6   'Legal Aid and Advice:
The Picture in Northern Ireland'
King, M.   LAG BULL. No. 5 p. 10   'McKenzie For Legal Aid'   McKenzie-
adviser and his potential role in obtaining aid for the unrepresented
defendant
Merricks, W.   122 N.L.J. 853   'Legal Aid – Quebec's New Plan'   Comparative
article on Quebec's establishment of new legal aid scheme
Samuels, J.   LAW GUARDIAN No. 84 p. 4   'Costs Against the Legal Aid
Fund'   A re-appraisal of the 1964 Act
Waters, R.L.   116 S.J. 384   'Legal Aid and the Industrial Relations Act 1971'
Wilkinson, K.H.P.   69 L.S.GAZ 368   'Divorce by Consent – Who Foots The
Bill?'   Notes that legal aid fund bearing brunt of funding these divorces
1973
Anon.   LAW GUARDIAN GAZETTE No. 89, p. 4   'Costs v. Legal Aid Fund:
an addendum'   Note on the consideration of Davies v. Taylor, O'Brien
v. Robinson and Shiloh Spinners v. Harding, on principles to be applied
in considering applications for costs out of legal aid fund, under 1964
Act

Anon. 70 L.S.GAZ 2081 'Legal Aid and Advice – 22nd Annual Report'
– LAG BULL. 71 'Civil Legal Aid and Advice – Sources' Sources – i.e. statutes and regulatons and a bibliography of textbooks
– 123 N.L.J. 141 'Legal Aid – Income Limits' Editorial on Lord Chancellor's Advisory Committee on Report of Law Society on operation and finance of legal aid system and its call for upward revision of income limits
– 117 S.J. 173 'Litigation Finance' Suggestion that Legal Aid Committees should look at likely outcome of any litigation (i.e. that cases may swallow up any possible damages awarded) in deciding whether to give aid
– 117 S.J. 233 'Legal Aid Costs' Unassisted (successful) litigants' costs from legal aid fund: Comment on Davies v. Taylor (No. 2); O'Brien v. Robinson (No. 2); and Shiloh Spinners v. Harding (No. 2)
– 117 S.J. 473 'Legal Aid Report' Comment on 1971-72 Report of Lord Chancellor's Advisory Committee. Deals in particular with liaison officer scheme
Field, F. 27 POVERTY 11 'Extension of Legal Aid to Proceedings before Tribunals' Statement of CPAG's case
Leach, P. 70 L.S.GAZ 1347 'Upper Canada Looks at Legal Aid'
Maidment, S. 123 N.L.J. 720 'Legal Aid in Matrimonial Causes' Reviewing problems of legal aid applications in matrimonial cases, and criticism of Law Society's attitude to such applications which still demand information about 'guilty parties'
Merricks, W. LAG BULL. 123 'Calculating Civil Legal Aid Eligibility and Contributions' (But note that on p. 123 the figure in item 8 should be 950-pounds, not 1250-pounds)
Pollock, S. LAG BULL. 264 'Legal Aid – The Criterion For Adjudication' A criticism of the criterion for granting/refusing legal aid which is based on hypothetical paying client; he discusses the 'reasonableness' test in s. 1(6), Legal Aid Act, 1949
Samuels, A. 123 N.L.J. 243 'Costs in Legal Aid Cases' Article setting out arguments as to how the costs system under the legal aid scheme could and should be improved and simplified. (Article also gives a list of articles published in N.L.J. and other legal journals in 1972 on this subject.)
– 117 S.J. 157 'Legal Aid: The Statutory Charge' 1949 Act: s.3(4). Article on the charge on person's property if he should fail to pay his assessed contribution
– 117 S.J. 198 'Legal Aid: Reporting Clients to the Area Committee' How solicitor should treat a client under legal aid scheme

Waters, R.L.   117 S.J. 316   'When Is The Grant Of Legal Aid Reasonable?'
S. 1(6) 1949 Act – when is it 'reasonable' for local/area committees
to decide not to give aid
White, R.   117 S.J. 883   'Being Reasonable About Legal Aid'   Reason-
ableness test for committees under s. 1(6) 1949 Act – reviewed
Vann, P.S.   123 N.L.J. 144   'The 1964 Legal Aid Act – Some Recent
Developments' A case by case analysis of the way in which the courts
have interpreted the 'just and equitable' provision of the Act which
allows defendants in real hardship to recover costs from the Legal Aid
Fund

1974

Anon.   138 J.P. 213   'Legal Aid and Advice'   Annual Report of Law Society
on Legal Aid and Advice summarised
–   138 J.P. 588   'Legal Aid: Separate Schemes'   Criticism of separate
development of civil scheme; criminal scheme; and new LAG-based
voluntary schemes, with little or no co-ordination between them
–   138 J.P. 658   'Legal Aid and Advice'   Short comment on early
appearance of Law Society and Lord Chancellor's Advisory
Committee's report on legal aid and advice – major recommendation
being that legal aid should be extended to representation in tribunals
–   71 L.S.GAZ 261   'Legal Aid 1972-73'   Review of 23rd Report on
Legal Aid and Advice
–   71 L.S.GAZ 1222   '24th Annual Report on Legal Aid'   (Editorial)
–   LAG BULL. 46   'Could Legal Aid Money Be Better Allocated?'
Economies by Government will inevitably take their toll on legal
aid expenditure.   Editorial asks if available funds could be better
spent
–   LAG BULL. 74   'Legal Aid Annual Stocktaking: A LAG Review'
Review of 23rd Report on Legal Aid and Advice
–   LAG BULL. 87   'Furnished/Unfurnished: Delay in Granting Legal
Aid Grounds For New Trial'   Case note on Johnston Investments Ltd.
v. Corriger (1973)
–   LAG BULL. 289   'Current Events in Legal Aid'   A review of the
24th Legal Aid and Advice Report 1973-74 (pub. November 74)
–   118 S.J. 173   'Legal Aid'   Lord Chancellor's Advisory Committee
23rd report on Legal Aid, · reveals work Committee at present under-
taking; also possible future areas of work
–   118 S.J. 317   'Costs and Legal Aid'   Stewart v. Stewart provides
material for those confronted with problem of legally aided wife
against unassisted respondent in a divorce petition

Anon. 118 S.J. 817 'Legal Aid' Lord Chancellor's Advisory Committee's Report for 1973-74. Recommendation that legal aid be available for tribunals. Editorial includes notes on possible cost; also noted increases recommended for legal aid limits.

Knott, E. 71 L.S.GAZ 1014 'Legal Aid Referral Lists: An Experimental Enterprise' Report of questionnaire on types of legal aid work done in one legal aid area

Miscellaneous 124 N.L.J. 398-419 'Legal Aid Special Issue' Contains articles on: practical advice on Legal Aid – Legal Aid Act 1974; the Legal Aid Annual Report; and Legal Aid Gaps and Priorities

Pollock, S. 118 S.J. 123 'Legal Aid: The Factor of Reasonableness' A reply to White, R. at (1973) 117 S.J. 883 (above)

Segal, D. 124 N.L.J. 159 'Representing the Poor: Developments in America' A comparative look at American provisions which could be instructive in the present debate over the adequacy of British schemes

Waters, R.L. 118 S.J. 231 'Legal Aid Act 1974'

1975

Anon. 72 GUARDIAN GAZETTE 1 '25th Legal Aid Report 1974-75'

– 139 J.P. 539 'Disparities in Legal Aid' Note on latest statistics

– 139 J.P. 594 'Legal Aid and Advice' Editorial comment on 25th Annual Report of Lord Chancellor's Advisory Committee

– 72 L.S.GAZ 1075 'Payments on account in Legal Aid cases' Law Society's proposed scheme

– 125 N.L.J. 1033 '25 years of Legal Aid' Editorial on 25th Annual Report on Lord Chancellor's Advisory Committee

– LAG BULL. 282, 284 'Groundwork for Reform' Editorial and summary of 25th Annual Report of Lord Chancellor's Legal Aid Advisory Committee

Harper, T. 125 N.L.J. 927 'Referral List' Note criticising Law Society proposals for a national referral list as a guide to individual solicitors' expertise

Merricks, W. LAG BULL. 258 'UnBritish?' Report of the Task Force on Legal Aid in Ontario, and its relevance to the British situation

Napley, D. 72 L.S.GAZ 970 'Legal Aid – 25 years on' Historical development of legal aid scheme, and assessment of present situation (complacent)

Seviour, S. LAG BULL. 188 'Legal Aid before the Commission of Human Rights' Explanation of system of free legal aid for individual complainants

Waters, R.L.   119 S.J.   819 'Legal Aid: Reasons for Refusal'

White, R.M.   20 JUR. REV.   233   'The Distasteful Character of Litigation
for Poor Persons'

(c)   CRIMINAL LEGAL AID

1970

Anon.   134 J.P. & L.G.R. 202   'Legal Aid – A New Survey'   Comment on
Cobden Trust's survey into how legal representation in criminal cases
operates

–   134 J.P. & L.G.R. 707   'The Legal Aid Scandal'   Criminal Justice
Act 1967 intended that part of cost of legal aid be recouped from
those who could afford it.   Reasons here set out why this intention
being frustrated

–   134 J.P. & L.G.R. 894   'Legal Aid in Criminal Proceedings'
Comment on survey by Borrie and Varcoe (below)

Borrie, G. & Varcoe, J.R.   120 N.L.J. 997, 1023   'Legal Aid: Criminal
Proceedings – A Regional View'   'I. Availability and Attitudes of
Courts'   'II. Contributions, payments on Account and Legal Advice'
Articles set out findings of survey which examines position of legal aid
in criminal proceedings in west Midlands

Cooke, B. CRIM.L.R. 485   'A View of the Contribution Aspect of the
Criminal Legal Aid Scheme'

Gleeson, D.P.   134 J.P. & L.G.R. 877   'Doubts and Enforcement of Legal
Aid Contribution Orders'   Enforcement procedures against those who
fail to make legal aid contributions

Morrish, P.J.   134 J.P. & L.G.R. 462   'A Criticism of Legal Aid in Criminal
Proceedings'

1971

Anon.   135 J.P. & L.G.R. 388   'Legal Aid – A Clerk Replies'   A justice's
clerk relates his own experience of the legal aid scheme

–   135 J.P. & L.G.R. 572   'Legal Aid Again'   Notes statistics on
criminal legal aid in 1970

–   68 L.S.GAZ. 188   'Criminal Legal Aid'   Editorial containing an
attempted clarification of the Lord Chancellor's address to the Law
Society of Scotland on this subject, which prompted much attention
and criticism

–   121 N.L.J. 471   'Legal Aid – From Those Who Hath Act'   Editorial
on effect of legal aid on delay in criminal courts

Anon. 121 N.L.J. 255 'Legal Aid in Magistrates' Courts' Comment on NCCL's figures for granting/refusing legal aid in London area magistrates courts

– 115 S.J. 373 Comment on Lord Chancellor's remarks that legal aid in criminal cases was too freely available, wasting public money in hopeless cases

Greer, D.S. 22 N.I.L.Q. 431 'Legal Aid for Summary Trials in Northern Ireland'

1972

Anon. 136 J.P. 108 'A Gap in Legal Aid' Suggests amendments in criminal legal aid scheme to deal with problems posed in obtaining statements of means from applicants who have mental disorders or contagious diseases

– 136 J.P. 123 'Legal Aid in the Crown Court' Comment on small numbers of contribution orders being made in certain crown courts

– 136 J.P. 499 'Legal Aid 1971' Statistics on grant of legal aid by magistrates' courts in 1971

– 116 S.J. 186 'Lawyer as Defence Champion' Note on Zander's survey of operation of legal advice for legally aided criminal in (1972) CRIM.L.R. (see LEGAL SERVICES)

1973

Anon. CRIM.L.R. 654 'Legal Aid in Criminal Cases' Editorial comment on recent criticisms of administration of legal aid system in criminal cases

– 137 J.P. 480 'The Future of Legal Aid in Criminal Proceedings' Comments on criminal legal aid, written in advance of Law Society's memorandum on this (reviewed at p. 506)

– 137 J.P. 506 'Legal Aid in Criminal Proceedings' Report of memorandum by Council of the Law Society to Home Secretary and Lord Chancellor

– 137 J.P. 617 'Abuse in Legal Aid Discretion?' Comment on Morris/Zander survey in L.S. Gazette (below) and reply to their criticisms of the allocation of legal aid cases to solicitors by magistrate's clerks in Inner London

– 137 J.P. 663 'The Clerk and the Socio-Illogical Survey' Response by a justice's clerk to some of the comments raised by Morris and Zander

Anon. 137 J.P. 658   'Legal Aid: A Survey Under Fire'   Editorial comment on Morris/Zander's survey, and David Napley's comments

– 70 L.S. GAZ. 2308   'Criminal Legal Aid in the Future'   Report of a memorandum by the Council of the Law Society

– 123 N.L.J. 690   'Legal Aid Proposals'   Comment on Report of Law Society Committee, chaired by D. Napley, on legal aid in criminal proceedings.   Their views were that there was urgent need to review working of current provisions for legal aid in criminal proceedings. Article reviews the proposals to deal with problems

– 123 NL.J. 899   'Allocation of Criminal Legal Aid Cases'   A review of an article written by Morris and Zander

– 117 S.J. 554   'Legal Aid in Criminal Proceedings'   Note on Law Society's memorandum to Home Office

Morrick, C. LAG BULL. 69   'Legal Aid in Criminal Appeals'   Sources of legal aid in criminal appeals – technicalities of Criminal Justice Act 1967 and legal aid regulations relevant thereto

Morrick, C. & King, M. LAG BULL. 215   'The Law Society on Legal Aid in Criminal Proceedings – Good in Parts'   Praise and criticism of Law Society's memorandum on legal aid in criminal proceedings

Morris, P. & Zander, M. 70 L.S.GAZ. 2372   'The Allocation of Criminal Legal Aid in Magistrates' Courts – A Study in London's Courts'   Article reviews legal aid powers and sets out statistics relating to actual state of affairs. Criticism of allocation procedures

Napley, D. 70 L.S.GAZ. 2358   'Who Decides, And On What Criteria, Policies For Allocation of Cases'   Editorial note on Morris & Zander's article

1974

Anon. 138 J.P. 2   'Costs for the Legally Aided'   Note on R. v. Arron (1973) 57 Cr.App.R. 834, which appears to run contrary to advice given to courts by Home Office circular on award of costs to legally aided defendants

– 138 J.P. 165   'Legal Aid in Criminal Proceedings'   The Law Society Memorandum scrutinized

– LAG BULL. 17   'Calculating Criminal Legal Aid Eligibility and Contributions'

Levenson, H. LAG BULL. 245   'Refusal of Legal Aid in Criminal Cases'

1975

Anon. CRIM. L.R. 286   Case-note on R v. Guildford JJ, ex p Scott Legal aid – committal proceedings – circumstances in which counsel should be assigned

Anon.   139 J.P. 158   'Counsel on Legal Aid'   Note on High Court guidance given in R v. Guildford JJ regarding justices' exercise of discretion under Legal Aid Act 1974 s. 30 to assign counsel under legal aid order

–   125 N.L.J. 145   'Right to Counsel'   Editorial on English approach to the right of a suspect in police custody to consult a solicitor typifying failure to protect individual rights, and comparison with Canada, where Bill of Rights operates

–   125 N.L.J. 882   'Costs: What the JPs say'   Editorial on recommendations on costs in criminal cases in magistrates courts made in Magistrates Association's Annual Report 1974/75

Finch, J.R.   139 J.P. 490   'How to tune the Legal Aid System'   Suggested reforms to achieve consistency and fairness in the system of legal aid in criminal proceedings

Harper, T.   125 N.L.J. 523   'Access to Solicitor'   Note on Access to Solicitors (Arrested Persons) Bill

Jackson, J.M.   125 N.L.J. 1158   'The Costs of Prosecution to the Acquitted'   Article on the costs suffered by people remanded in custody who are ultimately acquitted. A right to compensation is suggested

Levenson, H.   125 N.L.J. 1080   'Legal Aid and the Criminal Statistics'   Analysis of the latest figures (1974)

Teasdale, J.   125 N.L.J. 605   'Costs on acquittal in summary proceedings – A Note'

Zander, M.   CRIM. L.R. 364   'Legal Advice on Criminal Appeals: the New Machinery'

(d)   LEGAL SERVICES: GENERAL (and see: Law Centres, Duty Solicitors)

1970

Anon.   120 N.L.J. 999   'Unmet Need for Legal Services'   Short note on grant to Birmingham University to study unmet need for legal services in Birmingham area

Borrie, G.   LAW GUARDIAN No. 61 p. 13   'The Needs of Judicial Administration'   Describes scope of work of new Institute at Birmingham University

Townsend-Rose R.   67 L.S.GAZ. 49   'The National Legal Service'   Supposedly semi-humorous article on the possibilities of having a National Legal Service akin to the N.H.S.

Anon.   121 N.L.J. 1   'The Need for Legal Services'   Editorial gives details
of research project into need for legal services and indications in Law
Commission's 5th Annual Report for 1969-70 as to progress of these
projects, trying to assess the extent of unmet legal services

—   121 N.L.J. 309   'Legal Services: The Met Need'   Reiteration of
the classic arguments on unmet need for legal services, and comment
on Report of North Kensington Centre showing how great the need
is; statistics of work given

Hillyard, S. 68 L.S.GAZ. 31   'Legal Assistance Schemes and Local Law
Societies'   This article describes legal assistance schemes which are
being implemented by several local law societies to improve the legal
services offered in their respective areas

Samuels, A. 121 N.L.J. 111   'Do We Need a Ministry of Justice?'   Defects
in legislative process and administration of law give rise to this
question

Anon.   136 J.P. 371   'Access to a Solicitor'   Comment on Michael Zander's
survey and article on access to a solicitor in police stations in (1972)
Crim. Law Review

—   69 L.S.GAZ. 521   'The Right to See a Solicitor'   Editorial
comment on Zander's 'Access to a Solicitor in the Police Station'
(below)

—   69 L.S.GAZ. 921   'Legal Services and the Rule of Law'   Editorial
comment on Sir D. Heap's inaugural speech on this topic, to Law
Society

—   122 N.L.J. 111   'Legal Assistance – Local Schemes'   (and see
editorial comment at p. 93) Inquiry intending to reveal experience
of local schemes, and way in which this can be utilised to co-
ordinated schemes in best manner, to make use of manpower and
resources; includes note on Michael Meacher's Bill

—   122 N.L.J. 954   'L.A.G. – Return to Poor Man's Lawyers'
Comment on LAG Report: 'Legal Advice Centres – An Explosion?'

Brooke, R. 122 N.L.J. 687   'Information and Advice Agencies'   Results
of survey into various agencies for advice in urban areas in U.K.

Field, F. 24 POVERTY 9   'Establishing a free legal service for poor people'
CPAG memorandum to Lord Chancellor's Advisory Committee on
Legal Aid and Advice

Heap, Sir D. 69 L.S.GAZ. 435 'Inaugural Address by the President of the
       Law Society' Deals (amongst other things) with 'People and Legal Aid'
Levenson, H. 69 L.S.GAZ. p. 1112 'Trade Union Legal Services in Criminal
       Cases'
Mackirdy, D. LAG BULL. 8 'Welfare Rights in a Country District' Dis-
       cussion by a local solicitor who runs a social advice centre in Yorkshire
       of problems affecting this type of area
Zander, M. CRIM.L.R. 342 'Access to a Solicitor in the Police Station'
       The first assessment of available evidence on this aspect of the criminal
       law process
—   69 L.S.GAZ. 1238 'Informing the Suspect of his Rights in a Police
       Station' (with reply by Seton Pollock)

1973

Anon. LAG BULL. 20 'Costs for Solicitors as McKenzie Men' Case note
       on Malloch v. Aberdeen Corporation (1973) 1 W.L.R. 71 (H.L.)
—   LAG BULL. 138 'Who is To Run Legal Services?' Review of
       22nd Annual Report on Legal Aid
—   LAG BULL. 179 'Lay Representation' A consideration of the
       law's existing provisions for lay representation, in particular McKenzie
       v. McKenzie
—   LAG BULL. 210 'Getting the Clients to Solicitors' Editorial
       criticising present system of referral which fails to identify types
       of work that solicitors will undertake, and the difficulty that many
       individuals, particularly in poverty/welfare law field, experience in
       finding solicitors
—   LAG BULL. 238 'Legal Aid, the Community and the Lawyers'
       Report of discussion of this topic at the Law Society's National
       Conference, October 1973
—   123 N.L.J. 577 'A National Legal Service?' Editorial asks whether
       the ways in which aid and advice work, particularly for those living in
       poor areas and for cases of an 'unprofitable' nature, are satisfactory,
       and suggests that some of these problems could be overcome with a
       national system of legal advice centres in deprived areas
Brooke, R. 123 N.L.J. 211 'Demand for Legal Services' The author
       discusses the methodology used in the survey carried out in 1967/68
       by Abel-Smith, Zander and herself into the unmet need for legal
       services in poorer areas, and the relevance of those research techniques
       for future research into legal services
Coghlan, P.A. LAG BULL. 30 'A U.S. Legal Services Programme'
       Comparative survey of community legal service in Philadelphia

Corcoran, J. 7 LAW TEACHER 161   'Legal Aid – A Developing Need'
  Article on the Sheffield 'Free Legal Information Service' and general
  comments on unmet need for legal services and one town's attempts
  to deal with it

Field, F. 27 POVERTY 5   'Test Case Strategy'   Discusses early work of
  CPAG's Legal Department

Leach, P. 70 L.S.GAZ. 2210   'The Society Looks at Pre-paid Legal Services'

Lewis, R. & Latta, G. 123 N.L.J. 386   'Union Legal Services'   Provision
  of legal services by unions to members

Partington, M. LAG BULL. 75   'Getting Clients to the Lawyers'

Smith, J. 123 N.L.J. 1080   'A National Legal Service'   Article discussing
  criticisms of present legal service, working-class attitudes to lawyers,
  the provision of legal aid and advice centres in such areas; also criticizes the Law Society's and Lord Chancellor's Advisory Committee's
  recommendations for reform.   Presses the case for national legal
  service

Wegg-Prosser, C. 123 N.L.J. 1163   'An Effective Legal Service'   A reply to
  Smith, J. (above)

1974

Anon. 138 J.P. 239   'Legal Services'   Report on conference at Birmingham
  University April 1974 – deals (inter alia) with legal aid and its administration, representation before tribunals and duty solicitor schemes

—   138 J.P. 331   'Legal Services'   Comment on LAG's case for a
  'Legal Services Commission'

—   138 J.P. 350   'L.A.G. and Legal Services'   Reports LAG's work
  and publication of discussion papers on publicly financed legal services,
  pointing out defects and making recommendations

—   138 J.P. 635   'Legal Services'   Report of Lord Chancellor's speech
  at annual meeting of Paddington Neighbourhood Advice Centre on
  provision of adequate Legal services in social welfare field

—   71 L.S.GAZ. 288   'Legal Services – Government Aid'   Comment
  on Government's proposal to spend additional 50,000-pounds on
  centres to prevent them collapsing

—   LAG BULL. 70   'Stirring Times'   Editorial comment on developments in legal services and Lord Chancellor's speech demonstrating
  his intention of putting legal assistance and law centres as a priority

—   LAG BULL. 73   'A Preview of Government Policy'   Report on
  Elwyn Jones' speech on future of legal services in U.K.

—   LAG BULL. 77   'U.S. Notebook'   Short comparative survey of
  U.S. legal developments in the 'legal services' field

Anon. LAG BULL. 98 'The Distribution of Criminal Business' LAG's representations to the James Committee on proper legal representation in criminal business

— LAG BULL. 100 'Priorities in Legal Services: A LAG Report' Report of a special conference at the Institute of Judicial Administration

— LAG BULL. 122 'Proposal for a Legal Services Commission' LAG's proposal for a full and effective legal services commission in the future — submitted to the Lord Chancellor

— LAG BULL. 124 'The Lord Chancellor on Legal Aid and Advice' Report of Lord Chancellor's contribution to H.L. debate on 15/5/74 on legal services; particularly his emphasis on law centres

— LAG BULL. 202 'The Lord Chancellor's Package' Editorial assesses significance of Lord Chancellor's package on legal services

— LAG BULL. 286 'A Legal Services Commission Now' LAG again pressing case for Legal Services Commission, following latest rejection of this proposal by Lord Chancellor

— 124 N.L.J. 582 'Legal Services For The Future' Report on the LAG's call for a Legal Services Commission to ensure development of full and effective legal services in future

— 124 N.L.J. 781 'Unions and Legal Advice' The attitudes to legal aid and advice (editorial)

— 124 N.L.J. 731 'Small Earthquake at L.C.O.' Editorial comment on Government policies on law centres and financial provision for those in existence and further research into areas needing, but not getting, legal services

— 118 S.J. 409 'A Legal Services Commission?' LAG's proposals on setting up of such a commission reviewed

— 118 S.J. 485 'McKenzie Adviser' Note on their role

Archer, P. LAG BULL. 291 'Law and the Little Guy' Text of Archer's address to London LAG Group in September, 1974

Harvey, B.W. 118 S.J. 288 'Priorities in Legal Services' Report on Birmingham University's Institute of Judicial Administration annual conference

Hillyard, S. 71 L.S.GAZ. 36 'Current Developments in Legal Services — Part I' Outlines some recent developments in provision of legal services, especially to those not accustomed to consulting solicitors; also deals with legal research, legal aid scheme and advice centres

— 71 L.S.GAZ. 63 'Current Developments in Legal Services — Part II' Covers law centres, duty solicitor schemes and CABx

Leach, P. 71 L.S.GAZ. 452 'Legal Services for Poor People' This is a report of an American article by Samuel J. Brakel

Leach, P.A. 71 L.S.GAZ. 726   'Legal Services for People in Need'   Article
    on work of CABx. duty solicitors neighbourhood law centres with
    accompanying map showing location of all those in U.K.
Moore, P. 124 N.L.J. 868   'The Litigant's Friend'   Article on the
    'McKenzie Adviser'
Partington, M. 124 N.L.J. 236   'Some Thoughts on a 'Test Case Strategy' '
    Discusses different types of cases welfare lawyers may have to fight
Pitt, J. LAG BULL. 236   'A Culture of Silence'   Article argues that lawyers
    and other social workers in the community should make their skills
    available to the deprived and oppressed in a way that promotes self-
    reliance, rather than encouraging dependence
Pollock, S. 71 L.S.GAZ. 667   'Legal Services for the Future'   Critical
    review of LAG memorandum

1975

Anon. LAG BULL. 32   'FLIS'   Note on 2nd Report of Sheffield Free Legal
    Information Service
–   LAG BULL. 58   'A Divisive Memorandum'   Editorial on BLA
    memorandum relating to neighbourhood law centres: Independent
    Solicitors or a Second Best Service?
–   LAG BULL. 60   'Birmingham CAB's Solicitor'   Note on his report
    on first 15 months
–   LAG BULL. 143   'Umbrella'   Note on group of advice centres
    amalgamating to form Lambeth Umbrella Group
–   LAG BULL. 145   'Profile of a City'   Summary of some of the
    findings of research into legal services in Birmingham
–   LAG BULL. 170   'People and the Legal System'   Editorial on
    deficiencies of the system
–   125 N.L.J. 521   'Legal Services – a Stocktaking'   Editorial on
    results of study of legal services in Birmingham by Birmingham
    Institute of Judicial Administration
–   125 N.L.J. 570   'Community Centres and Rates'   Report from
    Newham Rights Centre on rate relief for financially ailing community
    centres
Allen, R. & Drabble, R. LAG BULL. 311   'The Free Representation Unit
    in Industrial Tribunals'
Bindman, G. LAG BULL. 177   'Private Practice: is it only for the rich?'
    Suggestions to encourage private practitioners to undertake more
    poverty law work
Browne, P. LAG BULL. 202   'Can I see a solicitor? It'll only take a
    minute'   Suggestions to enable private practitioners to help poorer
    sections of the community

36

Cain, M. 2 B.J.L.A.S. 61 'Rich Man's Law or Poor Man's Law?' Criticising the current emphasis of sociology of law on the area of 'poor man's law' to the exclusion of 'rich man's law', arguing that to understand and change society the study should encompass both

Dyer, J. LAG BULL. 7 'Why the poor don't go to law' A cautionary tale about an illegal eviction and subsequent proceedings, illustrating the effect of slowness of legal and administrative procedures on poor people, and the gulf that exists between them and the legal profession

Harper, T. 125 N.L.J. 79 'Leeds Advice Centre' Comment on this example of a free advice centre emerging to supplement official provisions where there is public need

– 125 N.L.J. 175 'Poppycock' Criticism of BLA memorandum which referred disparagingly to neighbourhood law centres: Independent Solicitors or a Second Best Service?

– 125 N.L.J. 223 'CAB Solicitor' Brief report of work undertaken

– 125 N.L.J. 423 'Administration' Note on Annual Report of Birmingham Institute of Judicial Administration

– 125 N.L.J. 543 'Passionate Patience' Criticial comment on Solicitor-General's address to LAG on availability of legal redress

– 125 N.L.J. 883 'Citizens' Advice' Note on National Association of CABx Annual Report

Harrison, R.F. 125 N.L.J. 276 'What now for lawyers?' How the legal profession must develop to adapt to changing requirements

Haslam, J.E. LAG BULL. 203 'Birmingham: the wider debate' Comments on research report on legal services in Birmingham (see LAG BULL. 145)

Hillyard, S. 125 N.L.J. 1045 'Providing Legal Services' Discussion of the legal services now in operation: CABx referral, duty solicitors, legal advice centres, law centres

Marsden-Smedley, S. LAG BULL. 204 'Lessons from Coventry' Discussion of papers on Coventry Community Development Project

Painter, A. 139 L.G.R. 599 'Trouble in the CABx' Article on the bleak future for some CABx, urging a re-think on funding in order to retain 'this valuable social asset'

(e)   LAW CENTRES

1970

Anon. LAW GUARDIAN No. 62 p. 3 'Advice Where Needed' Note on opening of North Kensington Neighbourhood Law Centre

Anon. 120 N.L.J. 675 'First Neighbourhood Law Centre East of D.C.' Note on opening of North Kensington Centre

— 114 S.J. 557 'Legal Assistance for All' Short editorial note on opening of North Kensington Legal Centre, its problems; comments on need for further and continued reform

Wegg-Prosser, C. 62 L.S.GAZ. 634 'The North Kensington Neighbourhood Law Centre' An examination of the Centre and its administration. More particularly, an examination of how far this Centre follows the pattern of the American Neighbourhood Law Firm as the local legal centre

1971

Anon. 121 N.L.J. 738 'Islington Legal Advice Centre' Short note on Centre and its work

Wegg-Prosser, C. 68 L.S.GAZ. 52 ' 'World-in-Action' Granada TV on the North Kensington Neighbourhood Law Centre' Criticism of the programme

1972

Anon. 136 J.P. 726 'Legal Advice — An Explosion' Report on LAG's report 'Legal Advice Centres — An Explosion'

— LAW GUARDIAN No. 85 p. 13 'Return to Poor Man's Lawyers' Comment on LAG paper: 'Legal Advice Centres — An Explosion?'

— 69 L.S.GAZ. 5 'New Legal Aid Centre in Westminster' Comment on decision to set up Paddington Centre

— 122 N.L.J. 93 'Legal Advice Centres' Comment on need for co-ordination in setting-up, manning and administration of these centres (see also, report of inquiry at p. 111)

— 122 N.L.J. 439 'C.A.Bx. and Legal Problems' Editorial raising problems faced by CABx., now in competition with other advice centres

Merricks, W. CIRCULAR No. 2, Feb. LAG BULL., p. 5 'Finance for Neighbourhood Law Centres' Discussion of sources of income for legal advice centres

Whetton, J. LAG BULL. No. 6, p. 11 'Following up Clients of Legal Advice Centres' Findings of research project on referral of clients to solicitors from legal advice centres

Anon.   137 J.P. 141   'Legal Advice and Assistance'   Report of Sir G.
        Howe's speech on opening Paddington Citizens' Advice & Legal
        Centre – his views on the subject
–   LAG BULL. 55   'Report of North Kensington Law Centre'
–   123 N.L.J. 1149   'Tom Thumb'   Comment on the problems,
        particularly financial, facing neighbourhood law centres.   Concentrates
        on North Kensington Centre and Sir Maltby Crofton's criticisms of
        left-wing tendencies in North Kensington Centre and his refusal to
        give aid to the Centre
–   117 S.J. 686   'Paddington Neighbourhood Law Centre'   Note on
        half-yearly report on Centre
Alcock, P.C.   92 LAW NOTES 295   'Sheffield's Free Legal Information
        Service'
Burkeman, S.   LAG BULL. 8   'CHECK! – A Rights Experiment on
        Merseyside'
Harris, F.   LAG BULL. 32   'The Neighbourhood andthe Lawyer'   Role of,
        and inter-action of, legal advice centres and community as a whole
Iller, M. & Bennett, N.   92 LAW NOTES 77   'Neighbourhood Law Centres'
        Article on the work of North Kensington NLC

1974

Anon.   LAG BULL. 2   'Should Law Centres Be Left To Die?'   Editorial
        comment on Kensington and Chelsea Borough's decision to discontinue
        finance to the North Kensington Neighbourhood Law Centre, and,
        in general, a comment on Government financing of such centres
Harper, T.   124 N.L.J. 562   Comments on North Kensington Law Centre's
        Annual Report for 1973 and LAG Paper on Legal Services
Leach, P.   L.S.GAZ. 726   'Legal Advice Centres and Neighbourhood Law
        Centres'   Article dealing with solicitors' rules regulating advertising,
        and Law Society waiver for solicitors engaged in legal aid work.   Also
        deals with centres and their work: types and how obtained.
        Examines relationship between solicitors and work of such centres
Wegg-Prosser, C.   71 L.S.GAZ. 875   'North Kensington Law Centre'
        Comment on North Kensington's Annual Report for 1973

1975

Anon.   72 L.S.GAZ. 315   'Brent Community Law Centre'   Summary of
        first Report

Anon. LAG BULL. 5   'Holloway Neighbourhood Law Centre'   Note on
       Report 1971-4
–   LAG BULL. 32   'First Report of Vauxhall Community Law Centre'
–   LAG BULL. 60   'Brent Community Law Centre'   Note on first
       Report
–   LAG BULL. 89   'Islington Law Centre Report'
–   LAG BULL. 174   'People and the System'   Extracts from first
       Report of Balham NLC
–   125 N.L.J. 72   'Liverpool Community Law Centre'   Description of
       work carried out by them
Harper, T. 125 N.L.J. 175   'Brent's Answer'   Comment on first Report
       of Brent Community Law Centre
–   125 N.L.J. 659   'An Appeal'   Comment on financial straits of
       North Kensington NLC
Leat, D. 2 BJLAS 166   'The Rise and Role of the Poor Man's Lawyer'
Lydiate, H. LAG BULL. 92   'What is a Neighbourhood Law Centre?'
       Description of Cambridge NLC
Prosser, C.W. 72 L.S.GAZ. 445   'A Plea for sense about Law Centres'
       Article attacking uninformed criticism of centres, and claiming that
       the demands on private practioners are likely to be increased rather
       than diminished as a result of the emergence of centres

(f)   DUTY SOLICITOR SCHEMES

1971

Anon. 68 L.S.GAZ. 539   'Duty Solicitor'   The JUSTICE Report on 'The
       Unrepresented Defendant in Magistrates' Courts'   reviewed (and see
       below)

1972

Anon. 136 J.P. 427   'Duty Solicitors'   Comment on the Bristol Duty
       Solicitor scheme
–   136 J.P. 518   'The Duty Solicitor of Bristol'   Emphasises role
       of Duty Solicitor and legal aid scheme
–   LAG BULL. No. 4, p. 3   'Duty Solicitor Schemes'   Report on
       Bristol Law Society's Duty Solicitor Scheme: first of its type after
       JUSTICE Report on 'Unrepresented Defendants in Magistrates' Courts'

Dent, R.   116 S.J.   724   'Bristol Duty Solicitor Scheme'

1973

Anon.   137 J.P.   114   'The Duty solicitor Schemes'   Note on Bristol and
          Cardiff schemes; also reported in LAG Bulletin No. 6
—   137 J.P.   334   'Two Duty Solicitor Schemes'   Short editorial note
          on Poole and Manchester schemes
—   137 J.P.   631   'Duty Solicitors'   Comments by a Metropolitan
          Stipendiary Magistrate at Magistrates' A.G.M. on duty solicitor scheme
Thomas, P.A. & Mungham, G.   70 L.S.GAZ.   2395   'Cardiff Duty Solicitor
          Scheme'

1974

Anon.   21 L.S.GAZ.   790   'Report of Sub-Committee Studying Duty Solicitor
          Scheme'   Deals with history, schemes, scope, problems and advan-
          tages
—   LAG BULL.   203   'Duty Solicitors: Where Next?'   Examination
          of duty solicitor schemes and suggestion of criteria with which duty
          solicitor schemes should apply
—   LAG BULL.   207   'Duty Solicitor Schemes: A LAG Report'
          Article outlines what such schemes set out to do, what they actually
          do, and how they are run
—   124 N.L.J.   627   Notes on adoption of duty solicitors in New Zealand
Jackson, M.H.   71 L.S.GAZ.   561   'The Hendon Duty Solicitor Scheme'
          Rather gloomy account of the Hendon scheme, frustrated by poor
          facilities
Palmer, K.A.   138 J.P.   373   'A New Duty Solicitor Scheme for Criminal
          Courts in New Zealand'

1975

Anon.   139 J.P.   56   'The Duty Solicitor at work'   Article reviewing
          experience of courts operating duty solicitor schemes
—   139 J.P.   377   'Duty Solicitors'   Note on Law Society broadsheet on
          duty solicitor schemes
—   139 J.P.   410   'Duty Solicitors at Marylebone'   Note on this scheme
          and Law Society's comments

Anon.   72 L.S.GAZ. 577   'The Law Society's Guide to Duty Solicitor
        Schemes'
–   LAG BULL. 198   'Guidelines for Duty Solicitor Schemes'   Editorial
        discussing Law Society's recommendation of minimum standards for
        such schemes
Finch, J.R. 139 J.P. 103   'Duty Solicitors – another view'   A less sympa-
        thetic view of the schemes in response to article at 139 J.P. 56
Harper, T. 125 N.L.J. 275   'Duty Solicitors'   Brief description of
        Cambridge duty solicitor scheme
Hillyard, S. 72 L.S.GAZ. 723   'Marylebone Duty Solicitor Scheme'   Half-
        term report
Hughes, R. 139 J.P. 131   'The Duty Solicitor at work'   Description of
        work undertaken by Cambridge Duty Solicitor
–   LAG BULL. 63   'Except in Cambridge'   Account of the Cambridge
        Duty Solicitor scheme
Stevenson, A. 72 L.S.GAZ. 317   'Duty Solicitors'   Support for duty
        solicitor schemes from member of City of Westminster Law Society

(g)   LITIGANTS IN PERSON AND UNREPRESENTED DEFENDANTS
       (and see Duty Solicitor Schemes)

1970

Anon.   120 N.L.J. 167   'Litigant in Person – Costs'   Comment on
        Buckland v. Watts (1969) 2 All E.R. 985 and Court of Appeal's
        refusal to allow costs to be awarded to litigant in person
Davies, C. 114 S.J. 502   'The Undefended'   Examination of unrepresented
        defendants in criminal cases and why they are undefended despite
        legal aid and advice schemes.   Proposals for reform
Harper, J.C. 33 M.L.R. 214   'Costs and the Do-It-Yourself Litigant'
        Account of Buckland v. Watts (1969).   Solicitor conducting his own
        case could claim costs for professional services reasonably incurred;
        lay litigant cannot

1971

Anon.   135 J.P. & L.G.R. 787   'Litigants in Person'   Note on Justice report
        on 'Litigants in Person'

Anon. 135 J.P. & L.G.R. 808 'Justice and Legal Aid' A retort to Justice's
findings on 'The Unrepresented Defendant in Magistrates' Courts'
– 68 L.S.GAZ. 540 'Do-It-Yourself Justice' Editorial on Justice
Report 'Litigants in Person'
– 121 N.L.J. 489 'Second Class Citizens in Law' Editorial comments
on 'Silent in Court' by Suzanne Dell, and Becker v. Home Office
(unreported county court case), lack of legal assistance and rights
of women – statistics
– 121 N.L.J. 919 'Litigants in Person – A Costs Anomaly' Comment
on Justice Report on Litigants in Person
– 121 N.L.J. 1037 'Unrepresented Defendants' Note on Justice
Report on 'The Unrepresented Defendant in Magistrates' Courts'
Justice 121 N.L.J. 936 'Litigants in Person' The Justice Report on
'Litigants in Person'; a summary

1972

Lewis, N. 35 M.L.R. 494 'Justice Reports on Litigants in Person and
Unrepresented Defendants' Review of the two Justice reports;
both reveal and emphasise problems in those areas, and lead to the
conclusion that greater infusion of salaried personnel into the legal
structure is inescapable
Zander, M. 122 N.L.J. 1041 'Unrepresented Defendants in Magistrates'
Courts, 1972' Results of survey into this question

1973

Anon. 123 N.L.J. 1102 'Litigants in Person (Costs) Bill' Note on Richard
Luce's Bill (editorial)

1974

Latham, C.T. 138 J.P. 428 'The McKenzie Friend' Discussion of
McKenzie v. McKenzie (1970) and qualifications which may be
necessary in applying this rule to present day magisterial practice.
(See also LEGAL SERVICES)
Samuels, A. 124 N.L.J. 579 'Costs of the Litigant in Person' Short
article on this subject – recent cases and bibliography

Anon.   72 L.S.GAZ. 181   'Lay Litigant's Costs'   Brief outline of Litigants
        in Person (Costs) Bill
–   125 N.L.J. 97   'Litigants in Person – Costs'   Editorial on Litigants
        in Person (Costs) Bill

(h)   LEGAL AID AND PRISONERS

1970

Anon.   120 N.L.J. 1195   'Legal Advice for Prisoners Denied'   Case of Gyula
        Knechtl (Editorial)

1971

Anon.   135 J.P. & L.G.R. 877   'Legal Aid for Prisoners'   Note on Cmnd.
        4846, which accounces Government's intention to liberalise practice
        relating to prisoner's rights to seek legal advice
–   121 N.L.J. 202   'Legal Advice – The Executive Looks After Its Own'
        Report of Select Committee on Parliamentary Commissioner and case
        of Gyula Knechtl. (Editorial)
–   121 N.L.J. 310   'Legal Advice for Prisoners Denied'   Comment on
        case of Gyula Knechtl and opportunities for prisoners to obtain legal
        advice
–   121 N.L.J. 1111   'Advice for Prisoners – 'Liberalising' Injustice'
        Editorial on Cmnd. 4846 which announced relaxation of prison
        rules allowing prisoners access to a solicitor
–   115 S.J. 937   'Legal Advice for Prisoners'   Note on Home Office's
        decision to allow prisoner who has suffered damage by alleged negligence
        by prison authorities, to consult a solicitor

1973

Anon.   LAG BULL. 243   'The Legal Position of Prisoners'   A discussion
        of the Prison Act, 1959 and Prison Rules 1964, 1968, 1971 and 1972,
        and the rights (if any) and obligations they may place upon prisoners

Zellick, G. LAG BULL. 186   'Lawyers and Prisoners' Rights'

1975

Anon. 139 J.P. 116   'Human Rights'   Note of Golder case at European
Court of Human Rights, which held that one of Britain's Prison Rules
contravened the European Convention on Human Rights
—   139 J.P. 451   'Prisoners' Rights'   Note on Home Secretary's action
giving effect to Golder decision, so that henceforth prisoners no
longer have to petition Home Secretary before engaging in civil proceedings
—   125 N.L.J. 589   'Prisoners' Rights — A Breakthrough?' Editorial on
discouraging decision in Fraser v. Mudge (1975) where CA held that
natural justice did not imply any right to legal representation in the
context of prison disciplinary proceedings
—   125 N.L.J. 783   'Ignoring the Umpire'   Note on Home Secretary's
implementation of ruling of European Court of Human Rights in the
Golder case, commenting on government's failure to accept Ombudsman's recommendation in earlier case several years before
Harper, T. 125 N.L.J. 1107   'Prisoners' Rights'   Note on Howard League
complaint to Council of Europe about changes made by Home Sec-
retary in Prison Rules, purportedly giving effect to Golder decision
Marriott, T.W. 125 N.L.J. 886   'Golder's case and the Interpretation of
Legislation'
Nash, W. LAG BULL. 175   'A Prisoner's right of access to a solicitor'
Consequences of decision in Golder
Zellick, G. 38 M.L.R. 683   'The Rights of Prisoners and the European
Convention'   Discussion of Golder's case on the rights of prisoners
to communicate with their lawyers

(i)   LEGAL COSTS: CURRENT PROBLEMS

1971

Samuels, A. CRIM.L.R. 409   'Costs for the Acquitted Defendant'   Examination of the position about costs for acquitted defendant contained in a (1959) Practice Note, and a proposal for a change

Anon.   123 N.L.J. 555   'Costs – A New Direction'   Comment on Practice
        Direction concerning costs, the effect of which is that defendant
        (acquitted) should only be deprived of costs when his own conduct
        has brought suspicion on himself, or when he has intentionally misled
        prosecution
–   123 N.L.J. 757   'Suitors' Fund'   Comment on Law Society's memo-
        randum on Report of Justice's proposal that a Suitors Fund be made
        available to mitigate hardship arising from court costs unnecessarily
        wasted
Samuels, A. 123 N.L.J. 487   'The Costs of the Innocent '   The acquitted
        and innocent litigant and his liability to pay costs
Thoresby, R. 36 M.L.R. 646   'Costs on Acquittal'   A comment on practice
        direction at (1973) 2 All E.R. 592, which has the effect of awarding
        costs to successful defendants in criminal cases
Wallington, P. 123 N.L.J. 126   'Costs and The Successful Litigant'   High-
        lighting disadvantages of litigants in person as regards costs; examples
Wegg-Prosser, C. 70 L.S.GAZ. 2270   'Proposals For A Suitor's Fund'
        Reviews of Law Society's and Justice proposals for a Suitor's fund

1975

Vann, J.C. 125 N.L.J. 539   'Covering Legal Costs'   Article on insuring
        against legal costs

(j)   LAWYERS AND SOCIAL WORKERS

1970

Anon. 114 S.J. 626   'Social Service Interlude For New Solicitors'   Short
        note on widening experience of solicitors
Glasser, C. 33 M.L.R. 547   Note on 'First P.I.B. Report on Standing
        Reference on the Remuneration of Solicitors'

Anon.   121 N.L.J. 285   'Thrice Into The Breach '   Editorial comment on
          P.I.B.'s 3rd Report (Cmnd. 4024) on solicitors' remuneration
–   121 N.L.J. 966   'Out On A Branch of Social Service'   Editorial
          comments on law's relationship to other social sciences
McGregor, O.R. 121 N.L.J. 624   'Law and Social Change'   General article
          on relationship of law to social sciences – contains discussion of
          poverty/welfare law area

Anon.   117 S.J. 153   'Welfare Law Practice'   Article on this includes advice
          centres, duty solicitors etc.
Brooke, R. 123 N.L.J. 63   'Solicitors and Welfare Rights'   Criticisms of
          solicitors' lack of ability to appreciate concept and nature of poverty
          law.   Author attempts to define nature of poverty law and types of
          work solicitors should familiarise themselves with in this area
Hodge, H. LAG BULL. 7   'The Solicitor's Place In Welfare Law'   Article
          indicating type of problems and law solicitor will have to familiarise
          himself with in welfare law area, especially tribunals
Howard, R. 117 S.J. 848   'Social Law'   Argues that there should be a new
          category of 'social lawyer' trained and recognised
King, M. LAG BULL. 60   'The Lawyer-Client Relationship'   Re-appraisal
          of traditional lawyer-client relationship in light of new social,
          economic and legal factors, such as legal aid, neighbourhood law
          centres, etc.
Williams, E.A. 117 S.J. 299   'The Solicitor and His Social Conscience'
          Praises modern solicitors.   Notes the charitable element in existing
          legal aid procedures
–   117 S.J. 540   'Slaves of Charity'   General article on legal aid and
          attitudes of lawyers to it
White, R. 117 S.J. 332   'Social Security: A New Field For Lawyers'
          Note on new field of work for lawyers generally

Anon.   CRIM.L.R. 415   'Unsupported Mothers and First Prison Sentences:
          An Exercise in Communications and Involvement Between a Probation
          Officer and a Social Worker'

Anon.   LAG BULL.   259   'Who Will Lead The Way?'   Editorial comment
on the Report 'Legal Studies In Social Work Education' (reviewed
at p. 279)

–   138 L.G.R.   590   'Law and The Social Worker'   Short note on report
issued by Central Council for Education and Training in Social Work,
that knowledge of law is essential for social workers

–   124 N.L.J.   258   'LAG – Advertising and the Practitioner'
Comment on Monopolies Commission's reference on solicitors' advertising.   LAG pressing for relaxation of Law Society's rules on this
to encourage solicitors to open in deprived areas and advertise their
services

Harte, J.   LAG BULL.   127   'Social Worker In A Solicitor's Practice'   A
London solicitor employs a social worker in his practice.   Article
explains his reasons

Harvey, A.   124 N.L.J.   869   'Legal Studies For Social Workers?'   Need
for social worker to be aware of legal matters and some technical
expertise in the poverty/welfare law field

Leach, P.   71 L.S.GAZ.   703   'Concerning Criticisms of Lawyers and the
Legal System'

Samuels, A.   138 J.P.   486   'Teaching Law To Social Workers'   Outlines
alternative views to those put forward by Central Council for
Education and Training in Social Work's Report   'Legal Studies
in Social Work Education' (noted at p. 452)

Weeks, A.   LAG BULL.   151   'A Citizen's Advice Bureau Worker's View of
Solicitors'

1975

Anon.   139 J.P.   152   'Law and the Social Worker'   Summary of Report of
Central Council for the Education and Training of Social Workers
from their study group on Legal Studies in Social Work Education

II   SOCIAL SECURITY LAW

(See also: Westergaard, pp. 18; 22-25; 74-77; 91-92 and Blackstone, Part 1, passim; ch. VII; ch. XIV)

(a)   SUPPLEMENTARY BENEFITS/FAMILY INCOME SUPPLEMENT

1970

Glasser, C. 15 POVERTY 11   'The Poor's Legal System'   The SB Handbook and SBAT system and procedure, and programme for reform (and see 18 POVERTY 11)

Meacher, M. 15 POVERTY 8   'Promoting the welfare of scroungers?'   The SB Handbook and standard control procedures on 'voluntary un-employment'

—   16/17 POVERTY 25   'Swings and Roundabouts'   Analysis of government's FIS proposals

Townsend, P. & Atkinson, A. 16/17 POVERTY 18   'The Advantages of universal family allowances'   CPAG proposals compared with government's new FIS scheme

Wynn, M. 16/17 POVERTY 23   'FIS and fatherless families'

1971

Anon. 1 FAMILY LAW 97   'Cohabitation'   Note on report by SBC

—   135 J.P. & L.G.R. 62   'Family Income Supplement Act 1970'

—   121 N.L.J. 381   'Supplementary Benefit Appeals'   New rules governing appeals in supplementary benefits cases — details

—   121 N.L.J. 441   'Co-habitation and Social Security'   Note of report (published by H.M.S.O.) on administration of s.4(2) and Sched. 2, para. 3 of Supplementary Benefit Act 1966 on co-habitation

Anon.   121 N.L.J. 716   'Supplementary Benefit – Appeals'   Review of
R.J. Coleman's study: 'Supplementary Benefits and the Administrative Review of Administrative Action' – CPAG (1971) – his study
of supplementary benefit appeals in 1968-69 with valuable statistics
–   18 POVERTY 14   'A plan to help the low paid and overcome family
poverty: Earned Income Relief'   CPAG memorandum to Chancellor
of Exchequer
Collison, Lord. 19 POVERTY 13   'Poor People's Rights'   Reply from
Chairman of SBC to criticisms CPAG made in 15 POVERTY of SB
Handbook

1972

Anon.   136 L.G.R. 572   'Welfare Visits To Supplementary Pensioners'
Comments on parallel responsibilities of SBC and local authorities'
social service departments in keeping pensioners informed of rights
and benefits and help available;   how system is running
–   122 N.L.J. 506   'Co-habitation – How To Do Injustice'   (Editorial)
Bear, C.R. LAG BULL. No. 6 p. 21   Review of 'The Penguin Guide to
Supplementary Benefits'   by Tony Lynes
Lister, R. 24 POVERTY 18   'The Earnings Rule'   NI Rules, and the
earnings rule for SB
Simpson, R. 23 POVERTY 15   'The Cohabitation Rule'   Summary of
CPAG's supplementary evidence to the Fisher Committee of Enquiry
into Abuse of Social Security Benefits

1973

Anon.   LAG BULL. 66   'A Beginner's Guide to Supplementary Benefits'
Good, simple, check list on this topic and simple advice on calculating
benefits
–   137 L.G.R. 864   'Law and the Welfare State'   Comment on power
of tribunals with regard to supplementary benefits and welfare law in
general
–   123 N.L.J. 309   'Come Back Pecksniff . . .'   Editorial criticism
of the Fisher Report on Abuse of the Social Security System, Cmnd.
5228, and the Government's reaction to it, in particular the 'snooping'
activities of the DHSS inspectorate

Burkeman, S. LAG BULL. 78 Review of 'Administrative Justice and Supplementary Benefits' by M. Herman; and 'Claimant or Client? A Social Worker's View of the Supplementary Benefits Commission' by O. Stevenson

Drabble, R. LAG BULL. 246 'Exceptional Needs Payments' ENP's (once off lump sum grants) to meet demands for exceptional expenditure

— LAG BULL. 200 'Exceptional Circumstances Additions to Supplementary Benefits' A discussion of the ways in which the SBC can increase a claimant's weekly benefit above the basic rates in circumstances where individual needs are high or exceptional

Hodge, H. LAG BULL. 47 'Cohabitation and Benefit' Analysis of the cohabitation rule (a frequent cause of distress and criticism, to claimants who have benefits cut off) and its application

Lewis, N. PUBLIC LAW 257 'Supplementary Benefits Appeal Tribunals' An examination of the work of these tribunals. The author's intention is to present a counterview to the theories and criticism of Professor Titmuss on the role of lawyers

Lister, R. 26 POVERTY 9 'Report of the Committee on Abuse of Social Security Benefits'

Moore, P. LAG BULL. 43 'Poverty Group Wins Appeal' Report on CPAG's appeal in R. v. Birmingham Appeal Tribunal, ex parte Simper

— LAG BULL. 176 'Students and Supplementary Benefit' Students' rights to supplementary benefit and circumstances in which they can claim

Moss, J. 137 L.G.R. 12 'From The Poor Law To Social Security, Health and Welfare' Tracing growth of state welfare system from poor law to present

Partington, M. 123 N.L.J. 449 'Students on Vacation and the Supplementary Benefits Commission' Article (written before detailed changes in the rules) attacked the legality of Supplementary Benefit administration on this issue

Reid, J. 2 I.L.J. 111 'Social Security — Strikes and State Benefit' Extended article on supplementary benefit and way in which it may be affected by worker on strike. Illustrations from decisions are given

— 2 I.L.J. 174 'Social Security — Report of the Committee on Abuse of Social Security Benefits — Cmnd. 5228' Full review of the Fisher Committee's Report

Samuels, A. 117 S.J. 516 'Family Provision' Family provision discussed in Millward v. Shenton (1972) 1 W.L.R. 711 where social security entitlement not taken into account. Cf. Re Canderton (1970) 114 S.J. 208 where Ungoed-Thomas J. said it was important

Schofield, J. LAG BULL. 272 'Supplementary Benefit for Students in Vacation Can Include A Rent Allowance' This represents a case-note of his findings, and the procedural complexity of the tribunal system after personal experience before tribunal

Smith, C. 123 N.L.J. 267 'Discretion Or Rule of Thumb?' Challenging the decisions of Supplementary Benefits Commission's officers in light of Simper decision; a criticism of certiorari as the best method of obtaining relief

— LAG BULL. 205 Review of 'As Man And Wife?' A Study of the Cohabitation Rule' by Ruth Lister (published by CPAG)

Weir, S. LAG BULL. 14 'Raising The Benefit Of Wage-Stopped Claimants' Minimum earnings rule and social security legislation which affects the level of benefits

— LAG BULL. 145 'The Wage-Stop' The concept of the 'wage-stop' as a bar to benefit, and its practical application. Article contains useful bibliography

White, R. 117 S.J. 332 'Social Security: A New Field For Lawyers' Article on the Simper case

1974

Anon. CRIM. L.R. 439 'Social Security' Case-note on Moore v. Branton obtaining benefit by false statement — mens rea required — s.29 Supplementary Benefits Act 1966

— LAG BULL. 84 'Supplementary Benefit: Or Rent and Rate Rebates?' Practical problems of claiming rent and rate rebates in conjunction with or instead of, supplementary benefit

— 124 N.L.J. 377 'Earnings Rule' Editorial on CPAG's call for review of earnings limits applied to supplementary benefit claimants for part-time work — two groups hardest hit — single-parent families and families with children still at school. Editorial supports CPAG's case and calls for reform of earnings rule

— 118 S.J. 394 'Social Security and Mens Rea' S.29 Supplementary Benefits Act 1966 and case of Moore v. Branton; wife claimed supplementary benefit but did not disclose that at weekends she shared with husband — in attempting a reconciliation of marriage; comment

Bradley, A.W. LAG BULL. 62 'Student Grants and Unpaid Parental Contribution'

Elks, L. LAG BULL. 134 'Supplementary Benefit And The Rent Stop' Article looks at use made by SBC of its powers to refuse to meet rents or mortgage commitments of claimants, when it regards these as being unreasonable

Elks, L. LAG BULL. 164 'Supplementary Benefit And The Rent Share' Description of effect of having a non-dependant in the home of a claimant who is rent-aided by SBC

Harvey, A. 124 N.L.J. 955 'Checking Supplementary Benefit' Position of wives in matrimonial cases with dependant children; importance of checking on their allowances

Hodge, H. 93 LAW NOTES 333 'Welfare Benefits' I – SB & FIS, and see (1975) 95 LAW NOTES 109 for II on rent and rate rebates, health benefits, local authority benefits

Jordan, B. LAG BULL. 300 'Urgent Need Payments' Supplementary Benefits Act 1966, s. 13

Lister, R. 29 POVERTY 27 'The Earnings Rule' Article reproduces letter arguing for a higher earnings disregard in SB assessment

Moore, P. LAG BULL. 14 'Maintenance, Affiliation and the SBC' An examination of the legal relationship between SBC, claimant and the court

– LAG BULL. 165 'Supplementary Benefit: Reviews and Late Claims' An explanation of the SBC's power to review decisions of the Commission of an appeal tribunal and circumstances in which late claims can be accepted

– LAG BULL. 183 'Voluntary Unemployment and the SBC' Techniques available to SBC to protect Exchequer from claimants who are alleged to be work-shy

Simpson, R. 28 POVERTY 18 'The Cohabitation Rule'

Smith, C. 124 N.L.J. 219 'Poverty Law: Discretion on Legislation' Article on issues raised in ex p. Simper (1973) and the National Insurance and Supplementary Benefits Act, 1973

Weir, S. LAG BULL. 81 'Householders, Non-Householders and Boarders' Article dealing with distinctions made by supplementary benefit scheme between householders boarders and 'non-householders'

Zara, R. LAG BULL. 16 'Family Income Supplement for Government Trainees' Case-note on a tribunal decision which established that F.I.S. can be paid to men undergoing Government retraining; thought to be first decision on this point

1975

Anon. LAG BULL. 33 'Abolishing the cohabitation rule' Note on CPAG memorandum

– LAG BULL. 119 'The Law of Social Security' Influence of EEC upon our national social security law, as shown by recent decisions

Anon. 125 N.L.J. 221   'Cost-effectiveness'   Editorial criticising present
       SBC policy regarding women on SB launching maintenance proceed-
       ings, and supporting Finer Committee's recommended unitary system
—   125 N.L.J. 1009   'Supplementary Benefit Appeals'   Editorial on
       Report of study carried out by Professor Bell on SB appeal system,
       based on tribunals operating in North of England, and summary of
       recommended reforms
—   119 S.J. 702   'Supplementary Benefit Tribunals'   Editorial note
       on Professor Bell's report
Bull, D. LAG BULL. 18   'Supplementary Benefit Appeals: Advocacy
       against policy decisions'   Account of successful appeals by SB
       claimant, their influence on policy changes, and lessons for advocates
Elks, L. LAG BULL. 124   'Family Income Supplement: Some Legal
       Problems'
—   LAG BULL. 319   'Supplementary Benefits: A new attitude to
       rents'
Grant, M. LAG BULL. 126   'Recovery of overpaid benefit'
Harvey, A. 125 N.L.J. 202   'Assessment of capital'   Assessment of capital
       for purpose of SB qualification
—   125 N.L.J. 703   'The scale rates'   The SB Handbook and scale rates
—   125 N.L.J. 814   'The Earnings Disregard'   SB system as it applies
       to part-time earnings
—   125 N.L.J. 1121   'Assisting the assisted'   Article about the rules
       for treating various kinds of income in the SB means test
Harper, T. 125 N.L.J. 79   'Cohabitation'   Brief summary of CPAG memo-
       randum calling for abolition of cohabitation rule
Hodge, H. 94 LAW NOTES 192   'Supplementary benefit — helping your
       client'   Guidance for solicitors
—   LAG BULL. 70   'Capital and supplementary benefit'   How capital
       is treated in the SB scheme, and common problems arising
—   LAG BULL. 158   'Income or Capital'   Decision in R v. London
       SBAT, ex p Taylor: gives guidance on whether arrears of maintenance,
       or other periodic payments, when received in a lump sum should be
       treated as income or capital for SB purposes
—   LAG BULL. 287   'Really: yet another tribunal?'   The shortcomings
       of SBATs, and proposals for urgently needed reform in the light of
       Professor Bell's report
McMahon, B.M.E. 38 M.L.R. 39   'The payment of supplementary benefit
       for strikers' dependants — misconception and misrepresentation'
       Article criticising and correcting pamphlet of Society of Conservative
       Lawyers: Financing Strikes

MacPherson, S. 5 FAMILY LAW 168 'Lawyers and supplementary benefits' A look at some aspects of SB scheme, particularly role of lawyers in advising and assisting claimants to these benefits

Partington, M. LAG BULL. 269 'Overpaid supplementary benefit and the Ombudsman' Article on two cases on overpaid SB which were referred to the Ombudsman

Reid, J. 4 I.L.J. 183 'SBC and Judicial Review' Case-notes on R v. Preston SBAT, ex p Moore and R v. Sheffield SBAT, ex p Shine

Saunders, I.A. 119 S.J. 618 'Supplementary benefits and grave financial hardship' Effect of Reiterbund v. Reiterbund (1975) and Dorrell v. Dorrell (1972) on scope of s. 5 of Matrimonial Causes Act 1972

Smith, C. 2 BJLAS 217 'Judicial Attitudes to Social Security'

Tunnard, J. LAG BULL. 184 'Mortgages and supplementary benefit' How mortgages are dealt with in the SB scheme, and problems

Whateley, C. LAG BULL. 237 'More on mortgages and supplementary benefit: raising a new mortgage'

(b)   NATIONAL INSURANCE LAW

1971

Anon. LAW GUARDIAN No. 72 p. 3 '1,250-pounds From Ministry' Case note on arrears of benefit ordered to be paid by National Insurance Commissioner to man who had claimed under s. 14 National Insurance (Industrial Injuries) Act 1965 (Special Hardship Allowance)

—   LAW GUARDIAN No. 74 p. 7 'What is Reasonable' Note on MacKenna J. in Eley v. Bedford (1971) 3 All E.R. 285 on social security benefits and special damages

—   121 N.L.J. 245 'Income Tax: Family Allowance 'Claw-back' Arrangements'

Munro, H.A. 121 N.L.J. 159 'Retirement Pensions After Divorce' Examination of financial problems of women over 60 when marriage ended by divorce; social security support

1972

Carson, D. 122 N.L.J. 973 'National Insurance Attendance Allowance — Appeals' Article on attendance allowances — critical of their technicality and appeals system

Denyer, R.L. 122 N.L.J. 543 'Special Hardship Allowance' S. 14 National Insurance (Industrial Injuries Act) 1965 and 'special hardship allowance'

Reid, J. 1 I.L.J. 49 'Social Security – New Legislation' Comments on:
National Insurance Act 1971; Social Security Act 1971, and F.I.S.
Act 1970

– 1 I.L.J. 109 'Social Security – Disablement Benefits' Case note
and analysis of the jurisdiction of medical boards and tribunals – in:
Jones v. Secretary of State for Social Security; and Hudson v. Secretary of State for Social Security

– 1 I.L.J. 252 'Social Security – D.H.S.S. Annual Report 1971'

1973

Hodge, H. LAG BULL. 269 'Welfare Law – Techniques For Tribunals –
Part I' Article describes situation that any representative is likely
to encounter, and techniques he may employ in supplementary benefit
tribunals, and National Insurance Tribunals

Lynes, T. LAG BULL. 38 'A Chart To Social Security' Chart of Social
Security benefits and all relevant literature, particularly DHSS leaflets.
Table of benefits included. (But NB: On the chart, family allow-
ances are not meanstested)

Munro, H. 123 N.L.J. 411 'The Golden Handshake' Examines taxation
and national insurance aspects of 'golden handshake' and attempts to
show impossibility of getting handshake without losing unemployment
benefit. (Article appears principally to concern higher-income bracket)

1974

Carson, D. 124 N.L.J. 142 'Attendance Allowances For the Severely Disabled' An examination of the technicalities of the National Insurance
Act and of some irregularities and anomalies that have appeared in the
course of tribunal hearings and decisions

C.P.A.G. LAG BULL. 133 'Tribunal Round-Up' A quarterly round up
of tribunal decision in the poverty/welfare law area

Drabble, R. LAG BULL. 295 'A Lawyer's Guide to National Insurance
Part IV – Unemployment, Sickness and Retirement: Some Questions
of Law' (See below for other Parts)

Hodge, H. LAG BULL. 13 'Welfare Law – Tribunal Techniques II' Part
II covers medical boards and medical appeal tribunals, and National
Insurance Commissioners

Mesher, J. 3 I.L.J. 118 'Social Security – Earnings Related Benefit'

Moore, P. LAG BULL. 240 'A Lawyer's Guide to National Insurance – Part
II: Some Overall Legal Concepts' This part deals with good cause
for late claims; overlapping benefits; due care and diligence to avoid

overpayment.   Moore discusses major rules common to whole scheme;
in particular those leading to disputes

Moore, P. & Drabble, R.   LAG BULL. 216   'A Lawyer's Guide to National
Insurance. Part I: A Bird's Eye View'   A wide ranging and fairly
exhaustive article on benefits, schemes, categories of claimant – in
effect, everything (including charts) on National Insurance

—   LAG BULL. 268   'A Lawyer's Guide to National Insurance. Part
III – The Remaining Overall Legal Concepts and Family Allowances'

1975

Anon.   LAG BULL. 122   'Digest of recent social security legislation'

Bell, K. et al. 3(4) & 4(1) BRITISH JOURNAL OF SOCIAL POLICY
'National Insurance Local Tribunals: A Research Study'

Carson, D.   LAG BULL. 67   'A Lawyer's Guide to National Insurance: Part
IV – Attendance Allowances'

Carson, D.   26 N.I.L.Q. 291   'The Attendance Allowance'

Drabble, R.   LAG BULL. 45   'A Lawyer's Guide to National Insurance:
Part V – The Industrial Injuries Scheme'

—   32 POVERTY 22   'Bars to Benefit'   Short account of these

Grant, M.   LAG BULL. 157   'Recovery of overpaid benefit – II'   Provisions relating to recovery of overpaid national insurance benefits

Ogus, A.I. 4 I.L.J. 12   'Unemployment benefit for workers on short-time'
Article seeking to provide a comprehensive but critical account of the
special rules governing   entitlement to benefit where the contract
of employment is not terminated but merely suspended

Reid, J.(ed) 4 I.L.J. 51   'Recent unemployment benefit cases'

—   4 I.L.J. 122   'Recent decisions on disablement benefit'

Sinfield, A.   32 POVERTY 10   'Benefits and the Unemployed'   Discusses
importance of getting case examples of how law works in relation to
the unemployed

(c)   MISCELLANEOUS WELFARE LAW ISSUES

1970

Anon.   134 J.P. & L.G.R. 581   'Local Authorities – Social Services Act 1970'

Atiyah, P.S. LAW GUARDIAN No. 60 p. 23   'Damages or Social Security?'
A reply to some of the critics of an earlier article written by Atiyah
on industrial injuries/damages systems

Brooke, R.   120 N.L.J. 728, 752, 779, 801, 821, 952, 999, 1060   'Social Welfare'   Series of articles on supplementary benefits;   Temporary Accommodation (Part III National Assistance Act 1948);   legal advice, supplementary benefit appeals;   reasonable rents;   social security and the disabled;   social security and the sick;   juvenile courts

Harris, J.   33 M.L.R. 530   'Local Authority Social Services Act 1970' Review article which includes some criticism of the chances of the Act fulfilling the aims of its authors

Moss, J.   134 J.P. & L.G.R. 601   'Chronically Sick and Disabled Persons Act 1970'

Thompson, B.   LAW GUARDIAN No. 55 p. 19   'Personal Injuries Litigation' A discussion between the alternative forms of compensation for injury at work: damages or industrial injuries benefits

–   LAW GUARDIAN No. 64 p. 21   'Compensation for Personal Injuries' Reply to Atiyah in (1970) L.G. No. 60, p. 23

1972

Anon.   69 L.S.GAZ. p. 749   'Interpreting Poverty Law'   Editorial

–   122 N.L.J. 907   'Tax Credits – The New System'   Appraisal of Green Paper – 'Proposals for a Tax-Credit System'   (Editorial)   See also p. 915

Fryd, J.   1 I.L.J. 61   'The Government's Pensions Strategy'   Analysis and criticism of Cmnd. 4755 which set out Conservative Government's plans for reform of pensions system

Williams, D.W.   122 N.L.J. 934   'The Great Tax Switchback'   Article on closer movement of social security and tax systems contained in the proposed tax-credit system

1973

Anon.   2 I.L.J. 116   Review of 'A Brief Guide to Social Legislation'   by N.J. Smith (pub. 1972)   Short review on this book, which contains an account of main provisions of welfare legislation in U.K.

–   2 I.L.J. 255   Review of 'Guide to the Social Services'   published for the Family Welfare Association.   'Book outlines provisions of law most relevant to social workers, including good sections on labour and social security law.   Highly practical in its approach, it contains the addresses of organisations and institutions engaged in the welfare scene'

Gilling-Smith, D.   2 I.L.J. 197   'Occupational Pensions and the Social Security Act 1973'   Review of Act in relation to development of company occupational pension schemes, and its control of standards of pension schemes

Meacher, M.   25 POVERTY 2   'The Tax Credit System – an opportunity lost?'   Summary of CPAG campaign on tax credits

Prest, A.R.   B.T.R. 6   'Proposals for a Tax-Credit System'

Reid, J.   2 I.L.J. 247   'Social Security – Social Security Act 1973'   Review of Act

Samuels, A.   70 L.S.GAZ. 2368   'Pensions – Social Security Act 1973'   Taxation aspects emphasised

Vann, J.C.   123 N.L.J. 1056   'Dual Pronged Pension'   Examination of the proposals for an earnings-related pension scheme in addition to the state pension in the Social Security Act 1973 – a measure to be introduced from April 1975.   (N.B.:   Now change of government.)   (This issue also contains two other articles on pensions by J.C. Vann)

–   117 S.J. 754   'What Lies Behind The New Social Security Act 1973'

1974

Berlins, M.   LAG BULL. 293   'Law Reporting And The Welfare Cases'   On necessity of lawyers engaged in interesting cases to let the press know

Harris, D.R.   37 M.L.R. 361   'Accident Compensation in New Zealand: A Comprehensive Insurance System'   An account of New Zealand legislation providing comprehensive insurance for accidents.   He notes that the proposals are revolutionary in terms of what accidents are covered and the fact that compensation is on a no-fault basis.   Finance, though, is still based on existing insurance schemes

Partington, M.   8 LAW TEACHER 135   'The Scope and Teaching of Welfare Law: Report of a Symposium'   On different possible approaches to teaching of the subject and the importance of starting courses

Smith, C.   118 S.J. 71   'What Is Poverty Law?'

Williams, D.W.   37 M.L.R. 281   'State Financed Benefits In Personal Injury Cases'   The article concentrates on recent changes in this field.   Examination of the 'overlap' between state benefits (for industrial injuries) and damages (i.e. via tort system)

1975

Industrial Law Society   4 I.L.J. 195   'Compensation for Industrial Injury'   Evidence of Industrial Law Society to the Royal Commission on Civil Liability and Compensation for Personal Injury

Hasson, R.A. and Mesher, J. 4 I.L.J. 168   'No-Fault – Private or Social Insurance?'   A revised version of the authors' evidence to the same Royal Commission

(d)   REPORTS OF WELFARE LAW CASES

There is no regular series of welfare law reports. However, CPAG in their Journal POVERTY and LAG in their BULLETIN have tried to bring together notes on particular cases of interest which have come to their attention. The following references refer to some of the notes that are currently available:

1970	1971
Brooke, R. 14 POVERTY 18	Anon. 19 POVERTY 17
	Lister, R. 20/21 POVERTY 28

1972	1973
Lister, R. 22 POVERTY 15	Lister, R. 25 POVERTY 24
– 23 – 23	– 26 – 20
– 24 – 26	– 27 – 20

1974	1975
Lister, R. 28 POVERTY 28	CPAG. LAG BULL. 98
– 29 – 32	– – 292
– 30 – 28	Lister, R. 31 POVERTY 42
	– 32 – 45

ADDENDUM

1972

Casey, J.P. 17 JUR. REV. 22   'Damages and Social Security Benefits – Recent Developments'

(See introduction)

(See also: Westergaard pp. 82-90, and Blackstone pp.58-60; 102-103; 110-120)

(a)   MAINTENANCE

1970

Cretney, S. 33 M.L.R. 662   'The Maintenance Quagmire' Examines problems, rights and obligations between members of family and those inter-family interests in the framework of the whole community. Goes on to discuss failure of law to take account of social policies it seeks to uphold
–   120 N.L.J. 267   'Maintenance: The Matrimonial Offence Preserved'
–   120 N.L.J. 288   'Maintenance: Magistrates' Powers'
–   120 N.L.J. 379   'Maintenance: Courts in Conflict – Judicial Realism'
Edwards, K.B. 120 N.L.J. 628   'The Matrimonial Proceedings and Property Act 1970'   I – Maintenance Orders
–   120 N.L.J. 652   'The Matrimonial Proceedings and Property Act 1970'   II – Maintenance Agreements
Gibson, C. 33 M.L.R. 63   'The Separation Order: A Study in Textbook Law and Court Practice'   A short study, with some statistical evidence of the use of the non-cohabitation (or 'separation') orders made by magistrates' courts under s. 2 Matrimonial Proceedings (Mags. Court) Act 1960
Samuels, A. 67 L.S.GAZ. 628   'The New Law On Financial Provision' Fairly detailed look at Matrimonial Proceedings and Property Act 1970. Highlights the problem of one man with one pay packet and two women to support

Anon. 1 FAMILY LAW 117 'Maintenance Orders – tracing defaulting bread-
    winners' Practice note
— 1 FAMILY LAW 161 'Maintenance by Post' Brief note on amend-
    ment to Rules re payment by post
Brown, G.G. 121 N.L.J. 516 'Grave Financial Or Other Hardship' S.4
    Divorce Reform Act 1969 – 'Grave financial or other hardship' What
    is it?
Earnshaw, T.K. 121 N.L.J. 856 'Conduct and Financial Provision' Conduct
    and its effect on financial provision to be made for wife under Divorce
    Reform Act 1969 and Matrimonial Proceedings and Property Act 1970
Lasok, D. 121 N.L.J. 1005 'The Illusion of Grave Financial Hardship'
    Financial hardship resulting from divorce and comment on Talbot
    v. Talbot (1971)

Bromley, P.M. 35 M.L.R. 625 'Maintenance Orders (Reciprocal Enforce-
    ment) Act 1972' Review of the Act designed to give greater financial
    protection to persons in U.K. when those liable to support are resident
    abroad. Something likely to increase with EEC entry
Earnshaw, T.K. 122 N.L.J. 705 'Polygamy and Matrimonial Relief'
    Article contains section on social security provisions on relief in a
    polygamous marriage situation
Samuels, A. 122 N.L.J. 864 'Matrimonial Law Financial Provision –
    The New Law' Matrimonial Proceedings and Property Act 1970,
    wide-ranging article on Act and some recent decisions on financial
    provisions

Bandali, S. 3 FAMILY LAW 165 'Maintenance Orders and Supplementary
    Benefits' Present law and proposals for reform
Glover, F.G. 123 N.L.J. 184 'Wilful Neglect To Maintain' A note ex-
    amining the meaning of the phrase 'wilful neglect' of a man to main-
    tain his wife – especially in the light of the decision in Brennan v.
    Brennan (1973)

Stewart, P.C.T. 123 N.L.J. 1132 'Maintenance – To, For or What?' The impact of the taxes acts on maintenance provision

Waters, R.L. 117 S.J. 757 'Liability to Maintain' Analysis of interaction between principles of family law and social security legislation

1974

Anon. 4 FAMILY LAW 169 'Maintenance and Financial Provision' Note on inconsistency in cases

– 138 J.P. 358 'Maintenance and the Ministry' Comment on two recent cases in Family Division – Billington v. Billington and Williams v. Williams – which explore the relationship between entitlement of state benefits on one hand and obligations of husband and father to maintain family on the other

Bandali, S. 4 FAMILY LAW 56 'Maintenance – relevance of conduct of parties'

Maidment, S. 4 FAMILY LAW 172 'Family Provision and the One-Third Rule' Purpose of article is 'to trace the origins of the one-third rule, to evaluate its present status, and to discuss its validity in terms of its rationale and justice'

Partington, M. 124 N.L.J. 467 'Divorce, Social Security and Legal Education' Note on implications of the Reiterbund case

Vries, E. de B.T.R. 201 'Tax And The Single Wife' A note on the changed tax liability introduced by the unified tax system, for those who recieve some maintenance payments

1975

Anon. 139 J.P. 393 'Maintenance and the Ministry' Note on effect of Jones v. Jones, concerning justices' power to determine reasonable level of maintenance where there is prior agreement between parties

– 139 J.P. 395 'The One-Third Rule' Implications of Brasman v. Brasman, which conclusively established the one-third rule as the starting point for the assessment of maintenance in magistrates' courts

– LAG BULL. 206 'Claiming Maintenance from abroad'

– LAG BULL. 320 'Separated wives and maintenance orders'

Bissett-Johnson, A. & Pollard, D.W. 38 M.L.R. 449 'Maintenance, Divorce and Social Security' Case-note on Reiterbund v. Reiterbund (1975) plus background

Latham, C. 5 FAMILY LAW 145   'Reciprocal enforcement of maintenance
orders in the EEC'

Parry, M.L. 125 N.L.J. 960   'Having regard to their conduct – financial
provisions on divorce'

Samuels, A. 5 FAMILY LAW 6   'Financial and property provision' Article
restating 'law, principles, practice and controversies' concerning
appraisal of material situation following divorce

Snow, P. 5 FAMILY LAW 72, 112   'Child of the family, liability to maintain, and Supplementary Benefit: Part I – effect and interpretation,
Part II – legislative history of provisions'

Strachan, B. 139 J.P. 241   'Recovery of maintenance abroad' Account of
the law governing this area

Waters, R.L. 119 S.J. 227   'Maintaining the wife' Maintenance cases:
discussion of Carr v. Carr – issue or whether court had power under
Matrimonial Causes Act 1973 s.35 to backdate any variation of maintenance agreement; Williams v. Williams – illustration of court's readi-
ness to accept an administrative decision of a government dept.

(b)   THE MATRIMONIAL HOME AND PROPERTY

1970

Kahn-Freund, O. 33 M.L.R. 601   'Recent Legislation on Matrimonial
Property' An article (partly comparative) principally concerned with
the Matrimonial Proceedings and Property Act 1970

Lever, J. 34 CONVEYANCER 383   'Matrimonial Proceedings & Property
Act 1970'

1971

Miller, G. 35 CONVEYANCER 332   'Expenses of the matrimonial home'
Article examining the position regarding payment of rates, mortgage
instalments and rent where a wife has been left in occupation of the
matrimonial home after divorce

Anon.   2 FAMILY LAW 57   'Mistress's Equity in prospective matrimonial
        home'   Effect of Cooke v. Head (1972)

–   122 N.L.J. 461   'Family Property: The Facts'   Comment on
        publication of Law Commission's report: 'Matrimonial Property'
        Intention of Report is to test how far suggested changes conform
        with social and economic realities

–   122 N.L.J. 485   'Legal Advice and the Home'   Light thrown on
        question of resort to legal advice in context of ownership and
        occupancy of home by the HMSO Report 'Matrimonial Property'
        (and see Legal Advice).   See also following editorial at p. 486: 'The
        Law: The Mirror of Life?' on same subject

Kahn-Freund, O. 35 M.L.R. 403   'Law Commission: Published Working
        Paper No. 42: Family Property Law 1971'   Review

Miller, G. 36 CONVEYANCER 99   'Trusts for sale and the matrimonial
        home'   Problems with trust for sale situation on breakdown of
        marriage, effect of Jackson v. Jackson (1971), and suggested reform

Polak, A.L. 2 FAMILY LAW 55, 93, 125   'Family Property Law'   On
        Law Commission Working Paper No. 42

Richards, M.E. 2 FAMILY LAW 27   'Evicting a spouse from the matrimonial
        home'

Richards, M.A. 2 FAMILY LAW 151   'The matrimonial home - further
        problems?'   Present law

Schofield, P. 2 FAMILY LAW 117   'Reforming the law of family property'
        Comments and some counter-proposals in relation to Law Commission
        Working Paper No. 42

1973

Cutting, M. LAG BULL. 165   'Some Legal Problems of Women On The
        Break-Up of Marriage'

Ellis, E. 3 FAMILY LAW 116   'Married women's property'   Interpretation
        in the cases of Married Women's Property Act 1964

Nevitt, D.A. & Levin, J. 36 M.L.R. 345   'Social Policy and the Matrimonial
        Home'   An argument for reform in rules governing ownership and
        occupation of the matrimonial home, so that clear basic rules are
        enunciated

O'Neill, P.T. 3 FAMILY LAW 150   'Property adjustment: Denning's dower'
        Long article on present law on property adjustment on divorce,
        drawing analogy with the law of dower

1974

Marshall, G.P. B.T.R. 30 'Some Economic Aspects of Family Property Rights Reform'

1975

Anon. 5 FAMILY LAW 66 'Married Women's Property' Note on Bothe v. Amos (1975) – wife claiming share in matrimonial home and in goodwill of business formerly carried on there by herself and husband
– 5 FAMILY LAW 102 ' 'Property' within the Matrimonial Causes Act' Note on Hale v. Hale (1975) – held that a weekly tenancy is 'property' within Matrimonial Causes Act 1973 s. 24(1)
– 5 FAMILY LAW 106 'Property adjustment after remarriage'
– J.P.E.L. 93 Case-note on Colin Smith Music Ltd. v. Ridge (1974) Rent Act – statutory tenancy – s. 3(1) (a) – mistress left in occupation
– 119 S.J. 37 'Matrimonial home: wife's interest extinguished' Brief comment on contrasting decisions of Cumbers v. Cumbers and Taylor v. Taylor regarding wife's interest in matrimonial home after short-lived marriage
– 119 S.J. 377 'A Mistress's Right' Brief comment on Eves v. Eves and Tanner v. Tanner, successful claims by mistresses in relation to properties formerly occupied during cohabitation
Bissett-Johnson, A. 125 N.L.J. 614 'Mistress's right to a share in the matrimonial home' Discussion of Eves v. Eves and Tanner v. Tanner
Chapman, V. 125 N.L.J. 20 'Improvements to the matrimonial home' Suggested approach to the quantification of the interest in the matrimonial home acquired by the improving spouse under s. 37 of Matrimonial Proceedings & Property Act 1970
Goudie, J. 125 N.L.J. 452 'Mistresses and the Rent Act'
Grant, M. 119 S.J. 670 'Council lettings and matrimonial jurisdiction' Implications of Thompson v. Thompson in context of general distinctions in matrimonial law between public and private tenancies
Jaffa, G. 5 FAMILY LAW 143 'Dividing the matrimonial cake' Problems when one spouse refuses to sell
Little, G. LAG BULL. 239 'Transfer of tenancies after divorce'
Parry, M.L. 5 FAMILY LAW 165 'Somewhere to live – excluding the husband from occupation of the matrimonial home' Wife's legal rights
Turner, J.M. 38 M.L.R. 397 'Confusion in English family property law – enlightenment from Australia?'

(c)   ONE PARENT FAMILIES (Finer Report)

1972

Brock, J. 2 FAMILY LAW 49   'Forward for the fatherless'   On NCUMC
memorandum to Finer Committee, commenting particularly on major
areas of law and income maintenance, and interrelation between social
security and familial rights and concurrent administration of these by
SBC and courts

1974

Anon. 71 L.S.GAZ. 673   'One-Parent Families And The Law'   Review of
Finer Committee's Recommendations
-        124 N.L.J. 639   'One-Parent Families – Finer Committee Recommendations'   Summary of Recommendations I
–   124 N.L.J. 669   'One-Parent Families – II'   Description of Finer
Committee's recommendations on income maintenance
–   124 N.L.J. 692   'Finer Committee Report: One-Parent Families'
Description of other recommendations
George, V. 28 POVERTY 2   'Social security and one-parent families'   The
failure of the present social security system to live up to aims of social
policy as outlined here, and basic principles for a new programme
Hill, R.N. 118 S.J. 706   'Maintenance Orders and the Finer Report: Some
Suggestions'
Streather, J. & Weir, S. 28 POVERTY 6   'Social insecurity: Single mothers
on benefit'   Harrassment, ignorance of rights, and necessary reforms
Polak, A.L. 4 FAMILY LAW 140   'The Finer Report on One -Parent Families'

1975

Anon. 72 L.S.GAZ. 311   'Supplementary benefit changes implement Finer
recommendations'   Practice note – SBC decision to ease conditions
under which claimants' rent may be paid direct to landlords
–   125 N.L.J. 53   'The future for family courts'   Editorial on Finer
Committee's recommendations for setting up family courts
31 POVERTY   Special edition on one-parent families
George, V. 31 POVERTY 6· 'Why one-parent families remain poor'   In-
adequacy of social security provision

Hall, J.G. 31 POVERTY 12 'Courts and one-parent families'

Harvey, A. 125 N.L.J. 480 'One-parent family concessions' Significant
    changes which have resulted from Finer report

Morrick, C. LAG BULL. 230 'What has happened to the family court?'
    Discussion of proposals for setting up family courts

Reid, J. 38 M.L.R. 52 'In the G.M.A. world' On the Finer Report

Streather, J. 31 POVERTY 2 'A Finer future for one-parent families'
    On the Finer Report

(d)   BATTERED WIVES

1973

Anon. LAG BULL. 159 'The Battered Wife – and More Reality' Editorial
    article highlighting some of problems confronting battered wives and
    difficulties in obtaining expert and effective legal assistance. (And
    see Legal Advice and Assistance)

Kesselmann, N. LAG BULL. 174 'Injunction for the Battered Wife'

1975

Anon. 125 N.L.J. 98 'Battered wives' Editorial on Battered Wives (Right
    to Possession of the Matrimonial Home) Bill

Greenberg, H. & Giller, H. 5 FAMILY LAW 68 'Common Sense for
    battered wives' Discussion of Brent v. Brent (1974) and Bassett
    v. Bassett (1974) which indicate the need to separate the procedure
    of getting an injunction from the enforcement of other legal rights

Harper, T. 125 N.L.J. 147 'More self-help' Brief comment on Cobden
    Trust pamphlet: Battered Women and How to Use the Law

Owens, D. 2 BJLAS 201 'Battered Wives: Some Social and Legal Problems'
    Description of the problems facing women in violent marriages, the
    extent to which the law is effective in solving these problems, and
    some suggested remedies

(See also: Westergaard pp. 14-15; 21-22; 99-109 and Blackstone: chapter XI, pp. 101-2)

(a)   HOUSING: GENERAL (including Housing Finance)

1970

Anon. 114 S.J. 1   'Rent Book Not Prerequisite'   A comment on C.A. in Shaw v. Groom (1970) and fact that landlords frequently do not comply with regulations governing rent books; legislation required to see that they do comply

Nance, J. 120 N.L.J. 7   'Distress For Rent – Replevin'   History and application of remedy of replevin

–   120 N.L.J. 148   'Covenants in Leases'   Provisional look at Law Commission's Working Paper No. 25 on this subject

1971

Wicks, M. 18 POVERTY 7   'Housing finance: the government's proposals and their implications'

Wylie, J.C.W. 22 N.I.L.Q. 389   'Leasehold (Enlargement and Extension) Act (N.I.) 1971 – A Critique'

1972

Anon. 136 L.G.R. 475   'Housing Aid'   Critical comment of Shelter's Studies of Housing Aid Centres

–   136 L.G.R. 497   'Advice to Tenants'   Note on Shelter's 'Security of Tenure and the Fixing of Rent' on tenant's rights

–   136 L.G.R. 790   'Reprieve'   Shelter Report on problems of multiple-deprivation areas and how to tackle them; comments

–   122 N.L.J. 70   'Tenant's Rights – The Integrity of the Law'   A comment on the relative deprivation of legal expertise, experienced by tenants in poorer areas

Anon.   22 POVERTY 1   'Fair deal for whom?'   Editorial on Housing
          (Finance) Bill
—   22 POVERTY 2   'The Housing Finance Bill'   Detailed analysis
Cheetham, T.   136 L.G.R. 276   'Housing Finance Bill — Ancilliary Matters'
Sherman, A.   137 L.G.R. 773   'The H.F. Act 1972 — Reflections'

                              1973

Anon.   9 COMMUNITY ACTION 35   'Better priorities'   Summary of govern-
          ment White Paper (Cmnd. 5339) on Housing
Bradshaw, J.   25 POVERTY 19   'Rate Rebates in England & Wales 1972'
          DoE Report
Brand, D.   11 COMMUNITY ACTION 28   'How to Appeal for Rates Reduc-
          tions'
Macintyre, C.   37 CONVEYANCER 11   'The Housing Finance Act 1972,
          Parts II & IV'
Merritt, E.P.   J.P.E.L. 154   'The Liability of Landlords for Nuisances
          Committed by Tenants'
Sedley, S. & Holmes, C.   LAG BULL. 111   'Law As A Tool For Tenants'

                              1974

Anon.   13 COMMUNITY ACTION 11 — 'New Rate Rebates'   Details of
          new scheme
—   16 COMMUNITY ACTION 17 — 'How to beat your meter'
          17   —   31   Two articles explaining individual's
          rights and how to use them in tackling gas and electricity boards,
          landlords etc.
—   LAG BULL. 244   'The Housing Act 1974'
Adamson, H.C.   71 L.S.GAZ. 845   'The Housing Act 1974'   Article on Act
Aldridge, T.M.   118 S.J. 618, 638   'Housing Act 1974'   Two-part review
          of Act
Brewer, I.   124 N.L.J. 968   'Resale of Electricity — A Current Problem for
          Tenants'   (And see Consumer Protection)
Hodge, H.   LAG BULL. 37   'Techniques Before Tribunals — Part III'   Deals
          with rent tribunals, rent officer and rent assessment committees,
          valuation courts
Othick, F.   138 L.G.R. 832   'Housing: Directors or Dictators?'   Examina-
          tion of Goodman's Dimbleby Lecture
Sherman, A.   138 L.G.R. 813   'Mr. Crosland's First Insight'

Sherman, A. 138 L.G.R. 836 'Goodmanship Examined Critically'
—   138 L.G.R. 852 'Mr. Crosland's Conversion System' Three articles
    on housing policy

1975

Anon. J.P.E.L. 316 'Current Topics' Note on DoE circular on 'Housing:
    Needs and Action'
—   J.P.E.L. 383 'Current Topics' Note on People and Homes, a
    report on landlord and tenant relations published by the British
    Property Federation
—   LAG BULL. 61 'Housing Aid Centres and County Courts' Note
    on suggestions sent by London Housing Centre Managers' Group to
    Lord Chancellor on how to improve liaison between housing aid centres
    and county courts
—   139 L.G.R. 167 'Housing Rents and Subsidies' Outline of pro-
    visions of Housing Rents and Subsidies Act 1975
—   139 L.G.R. 336 'Private rented accommodation' Review of
    independent study of landlord and tenant relations in England, 1974-
    75, People and Homes
—   139 L.G.R. 456 'Review of housing finance' Report of Environ-
    ment Secretary's address to Housing Centre Trust National Conference
    urging that a better system of housing finance must be found
—   125 N.L.J. 129 'Financial assistance for Housing Associations'
    Practice note on new bases on which financial support will be made
    available to housing associations in accordance with provisions of
    Housing Act 1974
Adams, J.E. 72 L.S.GAZ. 1028 'Mobile Homes Act 1975' Subtitled:
    'The Caravan-dweller's new charter — or not?'
Aldridge, T.M. 119 S.J. 194 'Housing Rents and Subsidies Act 1975'
Evans, D.L. J.P.E.L. 68, 457, 575 'The Housing Act 1974' Three articles
Green, G. & Stewart, A. 125 N.L.J. 400 'Why the Leasehold Reform
    Act is not working' Article on the 'shambles' of leasehold reform
Harper, T. 125 N.L.J. 611 'Landlord and Tenant' Brief note on Law
    Commission report — Obligations of Landlords and Tenants
Markson, H.E. 119 S.J. 174, 197 'Recent cases on general leasehold
    law'
McCall, P. 139 L.G.R. 733 'The housing mess — 1975 model' Attempt
    to identify some causes of the desperate housing situation, and to
    suggest solutions

Prichard, A.M.   39 CONVEYANCER 52   'Compulsory purchase and lease-
        hold reform'   Discussion of possible anomaly contained in Leasehold
        Reform Act 1967 where property coming within ambit of Act is
        subject to CPO
Smith, A.J.   72 L.S.GAZ. 513   'Housing Rents & Subsidies Act 1975'
–   72 L.S. GAZ. 1030   'Law Commission – Landlord and Tenant
        Law'   Summary of first of three Law Commission reports

(b)   LOCAL AUTHORITY HOUSING (and see Housing: General)

                                  1971

Anon.   136 L.G.R. 19   'Fair Rents – Fair Reimbursement'   Comment on
        default power if councils do not charge economic rents under Housing
        Finance Bill – criticisms of Act which places more strain on local
        authorities

                                  1972

Anon.   136 L.G.R. 135   'Assessing Fair Rents For Council Houses'   Note
        that under Housing Finance Bill assessment of council rents is to be
        by procedures adopted for private tenancies
–   136 L.G.R. 148   'A Social Injustice'   Short comment of Part V
        Housing Finance Bill which deals with assessment of fair rents for
        council tenants
–   136 L.G.R. 152   'What is Unfair About The New Housing Policy'
–   136 L.G.R. 205   'Council Fair Rents – A Consensus'   Opinion on
        fair rents in public, as opposed to private sector, based on review
        of 'Fair Rents For Housing Authority Dwellings' published by the
        Land Institute
–   136 L.G.R. 242   'Housing Finance Bill – The Subsidies'
–   136 L.G.R. 269   'What Is A Fair Rent'   Continuing discussion
        over fair level of rents to charge for council housing. This editorial
        gives some statistics from different areas of country to show existing
        extremes of rent
–   136 L.G.R. 305   'Local Authorities as Landlords'   Report on parlia-
        mentary debate which raised problem of differing attitudes by councils
        to tenants on security of tenure, eviction and whether reasons are given
Anon.   136 L.G.R. 309   'Assessing Fair Rents For Council Houses'   Supple-
        mentary to article at p. 135 (see above)

Shepherd, H. J.P.L. 197 'Roaring Inflation And The Implications For Fair Rents' Local authorities and Part V of the Housing Finance Bill

Sherman, A. 136 L.G.R. 114 'Council Housing – Second Thoughts' Questions value of council housing at all

– 136 L.G.R. 188 'Council Housing: Second Thoughts and First Principles' A reply to Aughton's article at p. 169

– 136 L.G.R. 312 'Lack of Thought on Housing' Vitriolic attack on Henry Aughton's article which contained criticism of Sherman's thinking on the economics of housing

Wilks, H.M. 136 L.G.R. 345 'Housing Bill – 1971 – Fair Rents'

Yates, D. 36 CONVEYANCER 402 'The protection of council house tenants – a melodrama in one act' Effect of recent legislation in the field of council house rents, and comparison of position of local authority tenant with private tenant

– 122 N.L.J. 983 'Security of Tenure and Council House Tenants I' Looked at in context of Housing Finance Act 1972 and White Paper 'Fair Deal for Housing'

– 122 N.L.J. 1020 'Security of Tenure and Council House Tenants II' Part II of the article deals particularly with possession orders, attachment and the case for security

1973

Aldridge, T.M. 70 L.S.GAZ. 1532 'Housing Finance Act 1972'

Bramhall, A. J.P.E.L. 142 'The Housing Finance Act 1972'

Sherman, A. 137 L.G.R. 371 ' 'Rights' and Duties' Problems in Kensington by influx of foreign workers who want housing and other social services. Sherman criticizes this trend and looks at duties 'inflicted' on local authorities by this trend

White, R. LAG BULL. 17 'Housing – Security: On Not Evicting Council Tenants' On Department of Environmental circular on practice as regards eviction of council tenants

Yates, D. & Holmes, C. LAG BULL. 170 'Local Authority Housing – Part I' Part I deals with responsibility of local authorities to provide housing and their selection of tenants

Yates, D. LAG BULL. 196 'Local Authority Housing – Part II' This article (Part II) deals with the nature of a council letting agreement

– LAG BULL. 249 'Local Authority Housing – Part III' Concluding article examines local authorities' duties to rehouse homeless

Yates, D. & Linden, J. LAG BULL. 198 'Security of Tenure' This discusses powers of local authorities to obtain possession orders

1974

Anon. 138 L.G.R. 891 'Housing Rents and Subsidies' Note on Housing Rent and Subsidies Bill (which, among other things, will repeal parts of Housing Finance Act, 1972 dealing with fair rents)

Gregory, R.P. 93 LAW NOTES 192 'Homelessness and local authorities' Extent to which homeless persons can make a claim on the public sector and demand local authority housing

Hackforth-Jones, C. LAW GUARDIAN/GAZETTE No. 101 p. 15 'Rent Acts and Local Authorities'

Harvey, A. 124 N.L.J. 541 'Local Authorities as Landlords' Local authority tenants; examples of local authority's power to evict etc.

Murray, J.W. 138 L.G.R. 888 'Housing Rents and Subsidies Bill' Report on parliamentary progress of Bill

1975

Anon. J.P.E.L. 530 Case-note on Bristol CC v Clark (1975) Local authority — statutory powers to evict tenant for arrears of rent

– 139 L.G.R. 74 'Rent Arrears' Note on the growing problem of non-payment of council rents

– 139 L.G.R. 90 'Local authority housing management' Comment on Environment Secretary's address to Institute of Housing Managers on importance of housing for rent, particularly council housing

– 139 L.G.R. 204 'Empty council houses' Discussion of the problem of empty council housing at a time of acute housing shortage

Webster, D. ROOF 7 'Council Home Costs: Why We should all Calm Down' Inflation temporarily creates large public housing subsidies, but in the long run reduces loan costs

Yates, D. 125 N.L.J. 873 'Evicting council house tenants' Article discusing possession actions for local authority dwellings in the light of Bristol CC v. Clark

(c)   REPAIRS, IMPROVEMENTS AND SLUM CLEARANCE

1971

Anon. 87 L.Q.R. 152 Comment on Buswell v. Goodwin (1971) concerning landlords who let their houses fall into disrepair

Anon. 68 L.S.GAZ. 51 'Law Commission Report on Defective Premises'
Comment

1972

Anon. 136 L.G.R. 412 'Housing Act 1969 – Part II' Note on Estates
Offices Ltd. v. Bebington Borough Council (1971) dealing with
keeping of houses subject to Rent Acts in a state of good repair and
providing them with standard amenities
– 136 L.G.R. 709 'Natural Justice And S. 16 Housing Act 1957'
An answer, and supplementary information to that provided in article
at p. 508 (by Burrell M.)
– 136 L.G.R. 996 'Another SHELTER Report On Slums' The
'Reprieve' Report (see also comment at p. 790) – a review and
comment
Burrell, M. 136 L.G.R. 508, 709 'Natural Justice And S. 16 Of The
Housing Act, 1957' Discusses requirements of notice in declaring
houses unfit under Act of 1957. Discussed critically in later article

1973

Anon. 9 COMMUNITY ACTION 3 'Mrs. Newton v. Nottingham Corpora-
tion' Background and account of legal battle over inadequate housing
(see also (1974) 13 COMMUNITY ACTION 3)
– COMMUNITY ACTION 'Action Report: How to Fight for Better
Housing Conditions' Special number
– LAG BULL. 199 'More On Specific Performance Of Repairing
Covenants' Case note on covenant to repair: Jeune v. Queens
Cross Properties Ltd. (1973) 3 W.L.R. 378
Evans, W.L.H. 123 N.L.J. 264 'Conditions on Improvement Grants' An
examination of the alleged abuse of the local authority improvement
grant system, which has allowed property developers to make quick
profits out of grant-aided schemes, and at the same time causes delay
and disappointment to individuals. The article aims to show how
local authorities could discriminate in favour of the owner-occupier
North, P.M. 36 M.L.R. 628 'Defective Premises Act 1972' A comment
on the Act
Oliver, D. LAG BULL. 64 'Housing Repairs and Amenities – Part I' A
series of articles on how to provide information on most effective ways
of getting a tenanted house repaired or improved. Part I: powers
and duties exercisable by local authority

Oliver, D. LAG BULL. 91   'Housing Repairs and Amenities – Part II'   More
on powers exercisable by local authorities

–   LAG BULL. 116   'Housing Repairs and Amenities – Part III'   Local
authorities' powers to have 'standard amenities' installed

–   LAG BULL. 142   'Housing Repairs and Amenities – Part IV'
Tenants' contractual rights against landlords when houses are in disrepair

–   LAG BULL. 168   'Housing Repairs and Amenities – Part V'
Problem of unwanted improvement and luxury conversions

–   LAG BULL. 218   'Housing Repairs and Amenities – Part VI'   Over-
crowding

Samuels, A. 37 CONVEYANCER 314   'Defective Premises Act 1972'

Sedley, S. LAG BULL. 173   'More On Using The Rent To Pay For Repairs'
Case note on Goff J. in Lee-Parker v. Izzett (1971) 1 W.L.R. 1688,
on the tenant's common law right to pay a reasonable sum for repairs
which landlord has failed to do and to deduct cost from future rent

1974

Reynolds, J.I. 37 M.L.R. 377   'Statutory Covenants of Fitness and Repair:
Social Legislation and the Judges'   An examination of the statutorily
implied covenants to repair imposed on landlords by the Housing Act,
1957, s. 6 and Housing Act 1961, s. 32. The author is critical of
judges who have failed to make the legislation as effective as it could
be

Sedley, S. LAG BULL. 161   'Setting Off Damages Against Rent'   Rights
of tenant to set off against rent any damages due to tenant for breach
of landlord's repairing or other covenants

Spencer, J.R. 33 C.L.J. 307   'The Defective Premises Act 1972 – Defective
Law And Defective Law Reform'   Part I of Article

1975

Anon. 20 COMMUNITY ACTION 13   'Action Report: Housing Action
Areas'   Description of Housing Act in Area Law under Housing Act
1974

–   J.P.E.L. 92   Case-note on Savoury v. Sec. of State for Wales (1974)
Clearance order – suitable alternative accommodation – Housing Act
1957 s. 42(1) proviso

Anon. J.P.E.L. 153   Case-note on Wolkind v. Ali (1974) Lodging house –
notice served under Housing Act 1957 s. 90 – limiting number of

persons per room

— J.P.E.L. 282 Case-note on Hunter v. Manchester CC (1975) Unfit house —clearance order — compensation — Housing Act 1969 Schedule 5

— J.P.E.L. 441 'Current Topics' Local authority housing obligations — note on Salford CC v. McNally (1975) — its implications for local authorities who use condemned properties as temporary housing accommodation

— J.P.E.L. 532 Case-note on R. v. Kerrier DC, ex p Guppys (1975) House unfit for human habitation — question of local authority's duty to take action

— 139 L.G.R. 89 'Housing action under the 1974 Act' Note on DoE circular giving guidance to local authorities on implementation of Parts I-IV of Housing Act 1974, discussing particularly housing renewal proposals

— 139 L.G.R. 251 'Unfit houses and nuisance orders' Comment on Salford CC v. McNally (1975)

— 139 L.G.R. 328 'Disrepair of council house premises' Comment on Brown v. Liverpool Corporation (1969) and Hopwood v. Cannock Chase DC (1975)

— 139 L.G.R. 393 'Slum clearance' Brief note on the change in policy from slum clearance to renewal strategies

— 139 L.G.R. 550 'Retention of unfit houses — compensation' Note drawing attention to DoE circular concerned with adjustment of compensation in consequence of decision to retain an unfit house

— 139 L.G.R. 617 'Unfit houses and nuisance orders' Comment on Salford CC v. McNally

— 119 S.J. 566 'Repairing unfit houses' Brief comment on R. v. Kerrier DC, ex p Guppys Ltd.

Garner, J.F. 119 S.J. 332 'Unfit houses in slum clearance areas' Article on points of legal interest raised by decision in Nottingham City DC v. Newton (1974), which decided that unfit houses under demolition order should be repaired pending slum clearance action — case also provides useful indication of powers of magistrates in making a nuisance order under Public Health Act 1936 s. 94 (see also 119 S.J. 482)

Hawke, N. 119 S.J. 482 'Unfit housing and nuisance abatement' Discussion of Nottingham City DC v. Newton

Markson, H.E. 119 S.J. 362 'Specific performance of repairing covenants' Discussion of provisions of Housing Act 1974 s. 125

Oliver, D. LAG BULL. 262 'Housing Strategies — 1' Series about areas of inadequate housing, and the powers of local authorities to treat whole neighbourhoods with the aim of providing better housing: 1 — sets out framework of law and policy within which a local authority decides how to treat a particular neighbourhood

Oliver, D. LAG BULL. 289 'Housing Strategies – 2' 2 – Housing Blight – features of blight and how to fight it

– LAG BULL. 314 'Housing Strategies – 3' 3 – Clearance Areas

Parris, J. 125 N.L.J. 516 'Grants under the Housing Act 1974'

Poole, F.T. 125 N.L.J. 653 'Liability of landlords for faulty flagstones and slippery steps' Effect of Brown v. Liverpool Corporation (1969) and Hopwood v. Cannock Chase DC (1975)

Spencer, J.R. 34 C.L.J. 48 'The Defective Premises Act 1972 – defective law and defective law reform' Part 2 of a long and critical commentary

(d) PLANNING, COMPULSORY PURCHASE AND COMPENSATION
1971

Tramah, D.A. J.P.L. 617 'Housing Act 1971'

Trice, J.E. J.P.L. 314 'Recent Development in Judicial Control of Compulsory Purchase Orders'

1972

Anon. 69 L.S.GAZ. 985 'Public Development – Compensating the Dispossessed' Comment on White Paper: 'Development and Compensation – Putting People First' Cmnd. 5124

– 69 L.S.GAZ. 1017 'Extended Compensation Rights for Blighted Properties' Further comment on White Paper

– 136 L.G.R. 540 'Compulsory Purchase of Houses for Rehabilitation' Comment on N.E. Islington Community Project on this and its urging of local authorities to make more extensive use of compulsory purchase powers against landlords who fail to provide decent accommodation for tenants

– 136 L.G.R. 741 'Compensation For Compulsory Acquisition and Planning Blight' A paper on this subject by UDC's Association, reviewed here

Adams, P.T. 136 L.G.R. 173 'Well Maintained Payment' Right to well-maintained payment under Housing Act 1957

Maybury, S.C. J.P.L. 1247 'Practical Difficulties and the Statutory Blight Provisions' Blight provision in Town Planning legislation, and the way in which its implementation can affect those most affected by the planning decisions

Moore, V. J.P.L. 673 'Development and Compensation – Putting People First' Cmnd. 5124

Robertshaw, P. J.P.L. 368 'Representative Amenity Actions by Local Authorities' An interesting note on s. 276 Local Government Act 1933, which provides that ' . . . when a local authority deems it expedient for the promotion or protection of the interests of the inhabitants of their area, they may prosecute or defend any legal proceedings'

1973

Anon. 9 COMMUNITY ACTION 13 'CPO's' Series of Action Reports on CPO's: Powers available, individual's rights, chart describing the process, compensation, council methods

10 COMMUNITY ACTION 15 The politics of CPO's, their misuse, non-use, and social and economic effects of implementation

11 COMMUNITY ACTION 17 CPO's for open space commerce and industry, and education

12 COMMUNITY ACTION 13 CPO's for Motorways and Roads

13   –   13 Review of rules relating to public inquiries

14 COMMUNITY ACTION 17 Tactics for fighting and hastening CPOs

– 70 L.S.GAZ. 1389 'Planning 'Compensation' ' Comment on 'Putting People First' – compensation for blight

Alder, J.E. J.P.E.L. 216 'Planning Decisions and Natural Justice'

Heap, Sir Desmond J.P.E.L. 201 'Ambience and Environment – The Shape of Things to Be' The 1973 Warburton Lecture

Joseph, C. 70 L.S.GAZ. 2029, 2052 'Land Compensation Act 1973' Two-part article

Moore, V. J.P.E.L. 71, 233 'The Land Compensation Bill' The Bill to give effect to Cmnd. 5124. Two-part article

Othick, F. 137 L.G.R. 428 'Putting People First' Note on Land Compensation Act

Samuels, A. 123 N.L.J. 556 'Land Compensation Act 1973' Comment on Act, which intends to deal with some of the problems posed by urban motorway construction

Trimble, W.D. 24 N.I.L.Q. 466 'The Procedure for Governing Compulsory Acquisition of Land in Northern Ireland'

1974

Davies, K. 38 CONVEYANCER 159 'Depreciation and disturbance compensation and the Land Compensation Act 1973' Background to Act, and its provisions

McAuslan, J.P.W.B. 37 M.L.R. 134 'Planning Law's Contribution to the Problems of an Urban Society'

Oliver, D. LAG BULL. 10 'Town and Country Planning 1974 Style: A Framework' A detailed synopsis of relevant and recent planning law and procedure, with the emphasis on advising clients involved in planning appeals and representations to local arthorities. Deals particularly with: planning authorities; the key planning concept, development; and planning permission, appeal and inquiries

— LAG BULL. 31 'Town and Country Planning: A Framework II' This article looks at development plans and how to influence them; and, in particular: the transition from old-style planning to new development, structure, and local plans. Also looks at issue of public participation

— LAG BULL. 52 'Planning Blight'

— LAG BULL. 104 'Compulsory Purchase – How It Works' Article describes how a compulsory purchase order is made, how it can be challenged, what compensation is payable, and what rights occupiers have to security or rehousing

— LAG BULL. 130 'Stop That Noise! Or Some Remedies for Nuisance' I Part I deals with 'neighbourhood nuisances' and remedies for this environmental problem

— LAG BULL. 152 'Stop That Noise! Or Some Remedies for Nuisance' II Part II – 'Is There a Motorway at the Bottom of your Garden?' Covers remedies available for environmental problems caused by public works such as roads and airports, particularly under Land Compensation Act 1973

Zetter, R. J.P.E.L. 515 'Planning Control and the Quality of Residential Environments' An account of the significance of Essex County Council's 'Design Guide for Residential Areas'

1975

Anon. 139 L.G.R. 394, 414, 444, 461, 510 'Compensation for compulsory purchase' Review of papers read at Law Society Conference

— 139 L.G.R. 702, 720, 734, 749 'Adequacy of the law of disturbance to meet actual losses when land is compulsorily acquired' Review of paper given at Oxford conference

Purdue, M. J.P.E.L. 445 'Natural Justice and the Post-Inquiry Procedure'

Samuels, A. 125 N.L.J. 239 'Compensation in a falling market' Argument that the decision in West Midland Baptist (1970) – that the time for assessment of compensation for compulsory purchase is the date of entry – must apply whether in a rising or a falling market

1972

Anon. 116 S.J. 702   'Immigrants and HousingLaw' Ugandan immigration spotlighted question of whether Rent Acts etc. needed revision for immigrants

1973

Anon. LAG BULL. 223   'Furnished Or Unfurnished – Inconsistent Decisions' Inconsistent decisions by County Courts on this topic – research results in London area indicate inconsistencies

Crane, F.R. 37 CONVEYANCER 233   'Rateable values and tenancies of dwelling houses'   Effect of Counter-Inflation Act 1973 and coming into force of rating revaluation on 1 April 1973 on groups of tenancies

Merricks, W. LAG BULL. 94   'Furnished Or Unfurnished'   Distinction Between 'Furnished' and 'Unfurnished'.   Article includes bibliography of articles and reports and cases relevant to the distinction

1974

Anon. LAG BULL. 55   'Furnished Or Unfurnished: Appeal Court Decisions' (Report)

–   LAG BULL. 211   'The Rent Act 1974'

–   118 S.J. 301   'Fewer Furnished Lettings'   Comment on Woodward v. Doherty

Adamson, H.C. 71 L.S.GAZ. 822   'The Rent Act 1974'   Lengthy article on the Act

Aldridge, T.M. 71 L.S.GAZ. 49 'Housing Musical Chairs'   Comment and review of Shelter's 'A New Deal For Furnished Tenants'.   Attempts to assess the report's objectivity and to bring some balance to its conclusions, since they may be open to bias

–   118 S.J. 602   'Rent Act 1974'

Arden, A. LAG BULL. 108   'Service Tenancies And Service Occupancies' Rules governing employee's occupancy of premises for purposes of his employment

–   LAG BULL. 155   'Tenant or Licensee?'   The difference explained

Partington, M. 124 N.L.J. 913   'Furnished Accommodation and The Rent Acts' Impact of Rent Act 1974 on Woodward v. Doherty

Poole, F.T. 124 N.L.J. 712   'New Crisis In Rented Accommodation' Note on Woodward v. Doherty and advice to landlords on how to get round it. (No mention of Rent Bill/Act 1974)

Samuels, A. 124 N.L.J. 924   'Rent Act 1974'

Street, H. 38 CONVEYANCER 394   'The Rent Act 1974: An Evaluation'

1975

Arden, A. LAG BULL. 73   'A note on attendances' Law relating to lettings in which attendances are provided

–   125 N.L.J. 681   'Holiday homes: tenancy or licence?' Analysis of the problem of the growing use of 'holiday lettings' to circumvent the Rent Act 1974

Paddington NLC LAG BULL. 101   'Residence: Attendances' Case-note on Ramakrishnan v. Hilton – successful application by tenants for declaration that their tenancies were protected – rejection of landlady's defence on grounds of residence and value of attendances upon tenants

Partington, M. LAG BULL. 100   'Holidays and the Rent Act 1974' The problem of defining a holiday letting

Prichard, A.M. 125 N.L.J. 100   'Rent Act Caprices' Article highlighting possible problems arising from Rent Act 1974

Samuels, A. 125 N.L.J. 80   'Residential tenancies: recent law'

Weir, S. ROOF 11   'Landlords Exploit Rent Act Loopholes' Account of abuses of the Rent Acts, particularly the 1974 Act, which have come to SHELTER'S notice

(f)   SECURITY OF TENURE

1970

Anon. 114 S.J. 517   'Tenant's Wife' Short comment on Penn v. Dunn (1970) 2 Q.B. 686 and positionof deserted wife of a statutory protected tenant

Baker, P.V. 86 L.Q.R. 16-17   Note on Foreman v. Beazley (1969) 1 W.L.R. 1387. Question of 'residence with' for purpose of deciding who could succeed to a statutory tenancy under the Rent Act, 1968. Differences in approaches by the courts noted

Anon.   LAW GUARDIAN No. 67 p. 5   'What About Case 8?'   A case note on
        Mykolyshyn v. Noah (1971) 1 All E.R. 48 on the circumvention of
        case 8 of schedule 3, Rent Act 1968
—   121 N.L.J. 37   'Landlord and Tenant — Suitable Alternative Accomm-
        odation'   Rent Act, 1968 s. 10(1).   Examination of Mykolyshyn v.
        Noah (1971)
H.C.C. 115 S.J. 166   'Protected Tenancy: Comprehension of the Rent
        Act 1968'   Criticism of the Act's wording and its reference back to the
        1965 Act.   This is important when it is realized that people most
        affected by Act's protection are often the least articulate
Powell-Smith, V. 121 N.L.J. 833   'Illegal Pruposes and Possession'   S.10
        1968 Act and situation in which certain of tenant's illegal activities
        may justify eviction

1972

Hoggett, B.M.   36 CONVEYANCER 325   'Houses on the never-never: some
        legal aspects of rental purchase'   Article discussing the issues as to
        possession and money claims likely to arise
Martin, J. 36 CONVEYANCER 266   'Contractual licensee or tenant for life?'
        Discussion of judgments in Binions v. Evans
Owen, E.C.H. 122 N.L.J. 719   'Landlord and Tenant — Forfeiture — Waiver
        and Relief'   Examination of question (i) waiver of forfeiture by un-
        qualified acceptance of rent with knowledge of breach of covenant,
        and (ii) relief against forfeiture for tenant in breach of covenant

1973

Aldridge, T.M. 117 S.J. 689   'Suitable Alternative Accommodation'   Note
        on Redspring v. Francis
Wilkinson, H.W. 123 N.L.J. 595   'Environmental Needs of A Tenant'   A
        comment on Redspring v. Francis (1973);   how courts have interpreted
        environmental needs

1974

Anon.   LAG BULL. 57   'Rent Act 1968.   Powers of Rent Tribunals To Give
        Security to Furnished Tenants'   (In Form Of Chart)

Anon. LAG BULL. 126 'Protection For Furnished Tenants' Views on Rent Bill

– LAG BULL. 277 'Rent Acts 1968 and 1974. Powers of Rent Tribunals to Give Security To Unprotected Tenants' Up-dating of table appearing originally at (1974) LAG BULL. 57

Arden, A. LAG BULL. 214 'The Rent Act 1974: Practice Note' 'Power to Rescind or Vary . . .' Examination of the power to rescind or vary an existing possession order which has not yet been executed

– LAG BULL. 302 'A Note On Statutory Residence' A note of Rent Act's 1974 introduction of 'owner-occupier' into landlord/tenant law

– 124 N.L.J. 957 'Power to Rescind Or Vary' Power to rescind or vary an existing possession order in 1974 Rent Act

Benson, G.N. 118 S.J. 195 'Protected or Not?' Meaning of 'dwelling-house' in Rent Act, 1968, s. 1 examined

Hoggett, B. 37 M.L.R. 705 'Relief For Rental Purchases – Equity Beats Parliament By A Short Head?' Case note on Starside Property v. Mustapha (1974) 2 All E.R. 567

1975

Anon. 119 S.J. 377 'Fettered Discretion' Brief comment on J. Sainsbury & Company v. Roberts concerning transitional provisions conferring discretion on court to rescind or vary unexecuted possession order made before Act came into force

Hoggett, B.M. 39 CONVEYANCER 343 'Houses on the Never-Never – Some Recent Developments' Follow up to earlier article by same author examining, in particular, problems relating to eviction, relief against forfeiture and money claims

(g) UNLAWFUL EVICTION AND HARASSMENT

1970

Anon. 134 J.P. & L.G.R. 939 'Harassment' Editorial comment on power of courts to deal with landlords who illegally harass tenants

– 114 S.J. 41 'Unlawful Eviction' Comment on protection afforded to a tenant by Warder v. Cooper (1970), unless landlord takes proper proceedings – unlawful eviction

M.S.G.   114 S.J. 78   'Furnished Statutory Tenant?'   Comment on ss. 30-
32 1965 Rent Act

1972

Anon.   CRIM.L.R. 318   Note on R. v. Abrol: case on harassment under
Rent Act, 1965, s. 30(2), and form of indictment required for that
offence
–   LAG BULL. 12   'Practice and Procedure in Harassment Cases'
(1) Part III Rent Act 1965   (2) Proceedings for an injunction
Strachan, B.   122 N.L.J. 758   'Protection From Harassment For Landlords?'
Effect on 1965 Rent Act re harassment and eviction – effects on land-
lords or superior tenants

1973

Anon.   137 J.P. 82   'Eviction and Harassment'   Note on circular (no. 15/73)
from Secretary of State for the Environment that penalties under s. 30
Rent Act 1965 for unlawful eviction or harassment, have been increased
by s. 30 Criminal Justice Act 1972
–   137 L.G.R. 102   'Unlawful Eviction and Harassment'   L.G. powers
to prevent unlawful eviction and harassment of tenants. (Short note)
Sedley, S.   LAG BULL. 89   'Injunctions in the County Court'   Article on
this topic, and argument for strengthening of power of injunction in
county courts, particularly in landlord/tenant cases

1974

Arden, A.   LAG BULL. 59   'Exemplary Damages in Eviction Cases'
Smith, J.   LAG BULL. 84   'S. 30 Rent Act 1965 – Remedies in Tort'
Argument that s. 30 implies remedy in tort as well as creation of criminal
offences of unlawful eviction and harassment

1975

Anon.   LAG BULL. 104   'Eviction proceedings in landlord and tenant matters
revisited'   Summary of law and practice

Holt, R.   LAG BULL.   15   'Can local authorities sue for harrassment?'

Anon. J.P.L. 269 'Rent Acts (Francis Committee's Report)' Minister's statement in House of Commons on Francis Report (short note)

— 135 J.P. & L.G.R. 588 'The Fairest Rent' Note on fair rents generally

— 121 N.L.J. 209 'Furnished and Unfurnished' Francis Committee on Rent Acts, Cmnd. 4609 — a review of the report

— 121 N.L.J. 233 'The Government's Reaction' Short report of Government's attitude to Francis Committee Report

— 121 N.L.J. 575 'Fair Rent Assessment — Procedure'

— 115 S.J. 177 'The Francis Report' This editorial is followed at p. 182 by a summary of recommendations of Francis Committee Report, Cmnd. 4609

— 115 S.J. 937 'Independent Rent References' Note on likelihood that local authorities will become more active in private housing sphere following C.A.'s decision in Frey Investments v. Camden Borough Council which confirms that in deciding to refer cases to a rent tribunal council did not have to take tenants' views into account

— 115 S.J. 494 'Fair Rent Where Tenant Not In Occupation' Comment on this problem, prompted by Feather Supplies v. Ingham (see (1971) S.J. 508)

Aldridge, T.M. 68 L.S.GAZ. 253 'Francis Committee Report' Argument that the Francis Committee should have upheld the case for assimilating the twin systems of furnished and unfurnished dwellings

— 115 S.J. 236 'Fair Rents Merry-go-Round' Emphasises the difficulty of setting fair rents in a market which has ceased to have any fair rent value since the 1965 Act virtually destroyed free market. A look at several assessment cases

Frazer, H.A. and Wylie, J.C.W. 22 N.I.L.Q. 99 'The Rent Restriction Law of Northern Ireland'

Powell-Smith, V. 121 N.L.J. 8 'Rent Control Proceedings' Examination of the Rent (County Courts Proceedings) Rules 1970, governing County Court procedure under Rent Act 1968 and Part III Housing Act 1969

Samuels, A. 68 L.S.GAZ. 282 'Rent Control In The Seventies' Intended to illustrate the drawbacks of the present system, and how reform should be channelled

— 115 S.J. 496 'The Fair Rent' What is the fair rent (s.46 1968 Act) — how is it calculated. (Bibliography attached to article)

Sophian, T.J. J.P.L. 262 'Valuation of 'Fair Rent' ' S.46(1) 1968 Act and the guiding principles established in Tormes Prop. v. Landau (1970) 3 All E.R. 653 (see also a letter at p.280)

Trice, J.G. 34 M.L.R. 427 'Report of the Committee on the Rent Acts' — Cmnd. 4609 Review of Report

1972

Anon. 136 L.G.R. 203 'Fair Rents For Furnished Dwellings?' Comment on news that DOE. Working Party set up to solve problems of extending fair rents principle to furnished tenants

Aldridge, T.M. 116 S.J. 46 'Problem of Fair Rents in Rem' Difference between maximum recoverable rents under controlled tenancies and fair rents payable under regulated tenancies, likely to prove problematic

de Smith, S.A. 35 M.L.R. 415 'Judicial Review and Administrative Discretionary Power' Note on R. v. Barnet and Camden Rent Tribunal ex p. Frey (1972) 2 W.L.R. 619. Analysis of 'relevant' and 'irrelevant' considerations of local authorities when they refer cases to rent tribunals

Glasser, C. & Thomas, P. LAG BULL. No. 5, p. 12 'Multiple References' A case note on decision in R. v. Barnet and Camden Rent Tribunal ex p. Frey (1972)

Partington, M. LAG BULL. No. 5, p.13 'What Is The Annual Rent For Students' Lodgings' Personal experiences of rent fixing by rent tribunals of a student's property

Samuels, A. 122 N.L.J. 572 'Landlord and Tenant – Block References to Rent Tribunals' Effect of C.A. in R. v. Barnett Rent Tribunal ex p. Frey (1972)

1973

Anon. LAG BULL. 18 'Housing – Rents: References By Local Authorities to Rent Officers' Power of local authority to refer furnished and unfurnished tenancies. Article outlines steps which may be taken to advise tenant in this situation. Gives references to appropriate statutory provisions and ministerial circulars

— 117 S.J. 802 'When Rents Need To Be Fair' Horford Investment v. Lambert and its failure to clarify effects of 1968 Act on sublet premises

Samuels, H. 117 S.J. 720 'Fair Rents v. Market Rents' In assessing fair rents, to what extent are market value and market rent relevant? And what is market value in this context? Article proposes to answer some of the questions that surround this topic

1974

Anon. LAG BULL. 107 'A Fair Rent – Sitting Tenant To Be Ignored'
Case note on House of Lords' decision in Skilling v. Arcari's Executrix
(1973)

– LAG BULL. 193 'Fair Rents – Comparables Still The Basis Of
Determination' Rent tribunal's reaction to Skilling's case (1974)

– 138 L.G.R. 891 ' 'Controlled' Into 'Regulated' Tenancies'
Technical note on The Regulated Tenancies (Conversion From Control)
(England) Order S.I. 1974 No. 1884

– 118 S.J. 353 'Rents: The Way Ahead' Comment on Government's
intentions for rent control in the future – equate position of furnished
and unfurnished tenants in Rent Bill

– 13 COMMUNITY ACTION 11 'Rent Freeze' Tenants' rights under
new counter-inflation measures

Robson, P.W. 118 S.J. 306 'Fair For Whom?' Reviews problem of assessing
'fair' rents and some recent authorities

1975

Anon. LAG BULL. 129 'Rents Now' Legislation affecting rents of different
tenancies

Aldridge, T.M. 119 S.J. 159 'Assessing fair rents'

Nicoll, R.C. LAG BULL. 244 'Fair rents for furnished accommodation'
Report of successful appeal by tenant against increase in fair rent

Partington, M. LAG BULL. 214 'Rent fixing: problems of jurisdiction'
Article arguing that Rent Officers can and should take difficult problems
of jurisdiction under the Rent Acts to the County Court

(i) ILLEGAL PREMIUMS

1971

Powell-Smith, V. 121 N.L.J. 207 'Illegal Premiums Again' S.85(1) 1968
Act. Review of cases up to and including Zimmerman v. Grossman
(1971) 1 All E.R. 363 on premiums on letting

Anon. 125 N.L.J. 758 'Consistency or Justice?' Editorial comment on
Farrell v. Alexander (1975) – loophole in s.85 Rent Act 1968 re illegal
premium

Arden, A. LAG BULL. 263 'Premiums' What constitutes a premium,
when it is illegal, and means of recovery

(j) ACCOMMODATION AGENCIES

1971

Anon. 68 L.S.GAZ. 355 'Accommodation Agencies' Article principally
concerned with problems thrown up by accommodation agencies,
the 1953 Act and the Court of Appeal's decision in Crouch and Lees
v. Haridas

1973

Anon. 117 S.J. 802 'Accommodation Agencies Again' Note on these
agencies and Lawrence and Another v. Sinclair-Taylor

Kerr, G. 24 N.I.L.Q. 1 'Estate Agents' Commission in Northern Ireland'

Moore, P. LAG BULL. 36 'Dishonoured In the Breach' Accommodation
Bureau charging fees – Accommodation Agencies Act 1953 – cases
on Act

1974

Anon. 124 N.L.J. 1117 'Accommodation Fees' Editorial comment on
Saunders v. Soper (H.L.)

– 118 S.J. 853 'Accommodation Agencies Clarified' Comment on
House of Lords' decision in Saunders v. Soper, which attempts to
clarify confused case law in area of Accommodation Agencies Act 1953

Anon. J.P.E.L. 152 Case-note on Saunders v. Soper (1975) Supplying of address by accommodation agency — money not recoverable where it is only due after client becomes tenant and in consideration of a tenancy being created

Holt, R. LAG BULL. 75 'When can accommodation agencies charge prospective tenants?' Effect of Saunders v. Soper

Partington, M. 125 N.L.J. 148 'Accommodation agencies and the law' Article considering interpretation of the Accommodation Agencies Act 1953 and suggesting reforms

Prosser, T. & Samuels, A. 72 L.S.GAZ. 514 'Accommodation Agencies' Provisions of Accommodation Agencies Act 1953, and suggested reforms

(k) RENT REBATES AND ALLOWANCES

1970

Bradshaw, J. & Wicks, M. 15 POVERTY 13 'Where have all the rent rebates gone?' The problem of poor take-up rates of rent rebates

Harvey, A. 15 POVERTY 5 'Rent allowances for whom?' Relevant considerations in assessing rent allowances

1972

Cheetham, T. 136 L.G.R. 224 'Housing Finance Bill — Rent, Rebates and Allowances'

Legg, C. 23 POVERTY 10 'Will rent rebates be claimed? The lesson from rate rebates' The failure of the rate rebate scheme suggests a similar fate for the rent rebate and allowance schemes unless the problem of take-up is tackled more resolutely

Sherman, A. 136 L.G.R. 693 'Rent Allowances To Furnished Tenants' (Taken from paragraph 2 of his article): ' . . . this is not a housing allowance, but an income allowance. It carries one stage further the onset of charity socialism, which ensures that people's income should bear no conceivable relationship to their earnings or contribution to society'

Anon. 137 L.G.R. 41 'Rent Allowances' Short note on rent allowances to people in rented, unfurnished accommodation under Part II Housing Finance Act 1972

– 137 L.G.R. 271 'The Furnished Lettings (Rent Allowances) Act' Note on Act

– 137 L.G.R. 372 'Rent Allowances – Furnished and Unfurnished Tenancies' Eligibility and problems of provision etc. under Housing Finance Act 1972

Aldridge, T.M. 117 S.J. 403 'Rent Allowances For Furnished Tenants' Deals with Furnished Lettings (Rent Allowance) Act 1973 – statutory instruments giving details of the scheme

Oliver, D. LAG BULL. 15 'Housing – Rebates – Poverty Law and Practice' Claiming and checking rent rebate and allowance – ss.18 and 19 Housing Finance Act, 1972

– LAG BULL. 118 'Rent Allowance For Furnished Tenants' Review of the Furnished Lettings (Rent Allowance Act, 1973)

Purnell, C. 26 POVERTY 15 'Means-tested benefit take-up among private sector tenants' Results of Survey

Wegg-Prosser, C. 70 L.S.GAZ. 1888 'Housing Finance Act 1972 extended to Furnished Tenants'

– 70 L.S.GAZ. 2180 'The Rent Rebate Act 1973'

Wicks, M. 25 POVERTY 17 'Rent allowances for furnished tenants' The Furnished Lettings (Rent Allowances) Bill – assessment

Anon. LAG BULL. 242 'Rent Allowances For Furnished Tenants' A detailed look at the way in which s.11 Rent Act 1974 brings rent allowance scheme for furnished tenants (protected and unprotected) into line with scheme for unfurnished tenants

– 138 L.G.R. 750 'Alternative to S.B.' Housing benefits (i.e. rent rebates, allowances) instead of supplementary benefit. The suggestions of DoE circular, 148/74

– 124 N.L.J. 875 'Rent Reliefs' Short note on work of Advisory Committee on rent rebates and rent allowances set up under Housing Finance Act 1972, s.23

Child Poverty Action Group LAG BULL. 79 Notes prepared by CPAG on Rent Act 1974's introduction of new rent rebate/allowance scheme Covers entitlement, calculation etc.

Anon.   139 L.G.R. 457   'Rent Rebates'   Brief note on eligibility for rent
  rebates under Rent Refunds (Housing Authorities) Regulations 1975
Elks, L.   LAG BULL. 233   'Rent rebates and allowances – some legal
  problems'   Legal problems thrown up by the scheme under the Housing
  Finance Act 1972
Ward, S.   ROOF 2   'Rebates 'trap' the low paid'   Note of the financial impact
  of rent rebates on the low paid

(l)   HOMELESSNESS EMPTY HOUSING AND SQUATTING

1970

Anon.   120 N.L.J. 745   'Homelessness and Order 113'   Squatting and the
  G.L.C. v. Lewis and Another (1970) case. (Editorial)
Coleman, R.J. & Scott, I.R.   134 J.P. & L.G.R. 364, 380   'Forcible Entry
  and Detainer: Substance and Procedure'   Two part article deals
  principally with criminal law in this area – emphasis on squatters,
  those who 'sit in' and those entitled to possession for purpose of
  evicting those who squat or sit in.   Special reference made to role
  of magistrates' court here
Goodman, M.J.   33 M.L.R. 281   'Adverse Possession of Land – Morality and
  Motive'   Article about the value of squatters' rights

1971

Anon.   135 J.P. & L.G.R. 115   ' 'Squatters' in Empty Houses'   Comment on
  Court of Appeal in Southwark L.B.C. v. Williams on squatters taking
  possession of council houses, showing that such persons are not in a
  position to invoke Part III of National Assistance Act 1948 that local
  authority shall provide temporary accommodation
–   135 J.P. & L.G.R. 589   'Homeless in London'   Extracts and
  discusses a number of points from Professor Greve's study, Homelessness in London, and a Working Party from DHSS on the same problem
–   87 L.Q.R. 151   Case note on Southwark L.B.C. v. Williams, (1971)
  2 W.L.R. 467. Squatting

Dashwood, A.A., Davies, B.J. & Trice, J.E. CRIM.L.R. 317 'Squatting and the Criminal Law. I. A General View' Part I of a series (by different authors)

Dashwood, A.A. & Trice, J.E. 121 N.L.J. 518 'Civil Dispossession of the Dispossessed' Courses open to property owners seeking to evict squatters

Davies, B.J., Dashwood, A.A. & Trice, J.E. CRIM. L.R. 342 'Squatting and the Criminal Law' Conspiracy to Squat

Maitland, R. CRIM. L.R. 337 'Squatting and the Criminal Law' Old Crimes with a New Image

1972

Anon. CRIM.L.R. 104 Note on R. v. Brittain: case on Forcible Entry Act 1381

– 136 L.G.R. 739 'Homeless Single People' Report issued by a Camberwell group on plight of single homeless particularly in Southwark

Gareth-Moore, E. 30 C.L.J. 17 'Necessity as a Defence' Note on squatting case of Southwark L.B.C. v. Williams (1971) Ch. 734

Hodge, H. 24 POVERTY 16 'Rights against homelessness' Squatters' rights

1973

Anon. 89 L.Q.R. 458 Case note on C.A. in McPhail v. Persons Unknown (1973)

– 137 L.G.R. 388 'A Sympathetic View on Squatters' Short anecdotal editorial note

Howell, T. 11 COMMUNITY ACTION 6 'Squatting' Short note on recent law by worker with Family Squatting Advising Service

Macintyre, D. 32 C.L.J. 220 'Squatters – Recovery of Possession' Comment on McPhail v. Persons Unknown (1973)

Watkinson, D. LAG BULL 74 Review of 'The Squatters' by Ron Bailey

Yates, D. 123 N.L.J. 763 'Squatters and Possession Orders' An examination of the precarious position of squatters, and the use of order 113 of Rules of Supreme Court, and in particular, McPhail v. Persons Unknown (1973)

Anon.   138 L.G.R. 113   'Local Authorities and the Homeless'   Review of
a Department of Environment/DHSS circular on central and local
government action on problem of homelessness

–   138 L.G.R. 395   'Squatting'   Local authorities and squatting
(G.L.C.'s situation in particular)   Asks what should their attitudes be

–   138 L.G.R. 415   'Local Authorities and the Homeless'   Follow up
to last item, on local authorities' responsibility to provide accommodation under s.21(1) (b) National Assistance Act 1948

Cutting, M. LAG BULL. 85   'Homelessness Now'   Examination of the
confused and uncertain situation at this time, of homeless people.
Article examines recent changes in law, local government reform
and Government decisions and their combined effect on this area

Green, W.A.   118 S.J. 124   'Legal and Illegal Squatting'

MacDonald, G.A.   71 L.S.GAZ. 899   'Law Reform: Squatters and Tres-
passers'   Comment on Law Commission Working Paper No. 54,
dealing with offences of entering and remaining on property

Powell-Smith, V.   124 N.L.J. 1012   'Some Aspects of Adverse Possession'
An article on squatters' rights in the light of two recent cases: Smirk
v. Lyndale Development Ltd. and Wallis's Holiday Camp v. Shell-
Mex (1974)

Sherman, A.   138 L.G.R. 893   'Britain's Housing Morass: Physical Squatter
Reflects Intellectual Slumdom'   Criticism of way in which housing
policy has been approached in last few years – characterised in
Housing: The Great British Failure by F. Berry, which Sherman
reviews

Watkinson, D. LAG BULL. 158   'Licensees Treated as Squatters'   Problems
of squatters reviewed, especially in light of decision of Pennywick J.
in Bristol Corporation v. Persons Unknown (1974)

–   LAG BULL. 304   'Licensees Treated as Squatters'   An updating
of his comments on Bristol Corporation v. Persons Unknown, with
comment on G.L.C. v. Jenkins (1974)

1975

Anon.   139 J.P. 83   'More Homeless, more in care'   Note on survey of
British Association of Social Workers

–   139 J.P. 112   'Empty Houses'   Note on address by Housing Minister
to Association of London Housing Officers on solutions to problem of
empty housing and the homeless

Anon. 139 J.P. 463 'Squatting' Note on Sir Robert Mark's statement on
Metropolitan Police's attitude towards squatting
– 139 J.P. 502 'Squatting and damage' Note on magistrates court
case, which held that the removal of a lock with intention to replace
it does not amount to 'damage'
– 139 L.G.R. 39 'Squatting' Note on the dangers of squatting to
local authorities
– 139 L.G.R. 106 'Empty houses and the homeless' Note on
Housing Minister's address – see above
– 119 S.J. 309 'Evicting squatters' Brief comment on decision
in Westminster CC v. Chapman
– 119 S.J. 513 'Effect of eviction' and 'Supplying squatters'
Comment on recent decisions: Rosenthal v. Flaherty and R. v.
Wandsworth County Court – both concerned with changes in occupation of premises during proceedings against squatters; Woodcock v.
SWEB – decided that when squatters occupy property they cannot
insist on electricity supply
Glover, F.G. 125 N.L.J. 813 'Eviction of Squatters – a note'
Harper, T. 125 N.L.J. 123 'Squatters' Comment on problem of securing
social justice for both squatters and owners
James, D.C. 38 M.L.R. 192 'Homelessness' Measures proposed in departmental circular on homelessness
Law Society 72 L.S.GAZ. 39 'Offences of entering and remaining upon
property' Memorandum by the Council's Law Reform Committee
and the Society's Standing Committee on Criminal Law on Law
Commission Working Paper No. 54
Markson, H.E. 119 S.J. 653 'Squatters' Brief general survey of law and
practice relating to squatters
O'Malley, S. 72 L.S.GAZ. 769 'Squatters Rights' Leader on the general
problem of squatting, urging that the Law Commission's proposed
criminal offence of being unlawfully on property should distinguish
between vandals and genuine homeless squatters
Robertson, G. LAG BULL. 11 'The Selsdon Spirit' Article commenting
on Law Commission Working Paper 54: Offences of Entering and
Remaining on Property
Samuels, A. 125 N.L.J. 5 'Entering and remaining upon property' Critical
discussion of Law Commission Working Paper 54
Sherman, A. 139 L.G.R. 509 'Squatters – symbols of our age' Attack on
the 'growth industry' of squatting which, together with the reluctance
to use police powers to enforce law and order , is a symptom of the
continuing breakdown of our society. See also ibid, p. 763

Teasdale, J. 125 N.L.J. 949   'Rules are made to be broken: recent squatting
  decisions'
Watkinson, D. LAG BULL. 13 'Advising squatters' The law relating to
  squatters, in question and answer form

V   CONSUMER LAW

(a)   CONSUMER PROTECTION: GENERAL AND MISCELLANEOUS

1970

Anon. 120 N.L.J. 213   'Conveyancing And The Consumer'   Review of
  'Which?' Report (1970) on conveyancing. See also p. 234

1971

Anon. 135 J.P. & L.G.R. 538   'Unsolicited Goods and Services'   Comment
  on Unsolicited Goods and Services Act 1971
—   115 S.J. 533   'Unsolicited Goods'   Short editorial comment on
  some of the problems solved by the Act
Samuels, A. 115 S.J. 536   'Unsolicited Goods and Services Act 1971' .

1972

Anon. 136 L.G.R. 149   'Local Authorities and Legal Advice'   Comment
  on connection between local authorities and Citizens Advice Bureaux
  particularly in Trade Descriptions field
—   136 L.G.R. 409   'Consumer Advice Centres'   Commenting on
  Council's attitudes to such centres as suggested by Consumer Council
  in 'Which?'
—   136 L.G.R. 642   'Consumer Protection'   Comments on proposals
  forwarded to a Law Society Commerce and Industry Group conference
  on this topic — emphasis local enforcement and local authorities' role
—   136 L.G.R. 729   'French Consumer Protection'   Comparative view
  on this topic
Brough, E. 69 L.S.GAZ. p. 1235   'Industrial Responsibilities Towards the
  Consumer'   Paper by Director of Unilever Ltd. on industrialists'
  responsibilities to consumer
Loosemoore, J. 69 L.S.GAZ. No. 6 p. 12   'Unsolicited Goods and Services
  Act 1971'

Anon. 123 N.L.J. 685   'Consumer Protection and the Law'   Contains
    verbatim extracts from Sir G. Howe's speech to Justice on 26/6/73
    on consumer protection
— 117 S.J. 765   'Fair Trading and Legal Aid'
Adamson, H.C. 70 L.S.GAZ. 1779   'Trade Directory Entries and the Unsol-
    icited Goods and Services Act 1971'
Green, A. LAG BULL. 224   'Consumer Rights — Recent Consumer Legis-
    lation'   Discussion of consumer protection law in Sale of Goods
    (Implied Terms) Act 1971 and Fair Trading Act 1973
Horsfall-Turner, H. 70 L.S.GAZ. 2498   'Foreshadowed Changes in Com-
    plaints Procedure'   Revision of complaints procedure, due to Govern-
    ment's decision to exclude professions from scrutiny under Fair
    Trading Bill
Hosker, J. LAG BULL. 62   'Local Consumer Advice Centre'   Pattern and
    working of Consumer's Association Consumer Advice Centres; lessons
    to be learned and their possible future under local authority control
Kahn, E. 137 J.P. 354   'Consumer Protection'   Comparative article on
    South African situtation
Passingham, B. 70 L.S.GAZ. 2060   'The Supply of Goods (Implied Terms)
    Act 1971'
Powles, D.G. 123 N.L.J. 624   'Misrepresentation Act 1967 — Six Years On'
Ryan, C.J.L. 117 S.J. 363   'Supply of Goods (Implied Terms) Act 1973'
Samuels, A. 117 S.J. 753   'Fair Trading Act 1973'
Yates, D. 123 N.L.J. 59   'Merchantable Quality and Consumer Protection'
    Aim of article is to examine contracts for sale of goods in light of
    consumer's expectations under that contract. Article examines major
    cases in particular Ashington Piggeries v. Christopher Hill

1974

Anon. 138 L.G.R. 37   'Enforcing Fair Trading'   Short note on local author-
    ities' obligations and duties of enforcement in consumer legislation
— 138 L.G.R. 203   'Consumer Protection and Advice'   Local author-
    ities setting up Citizens Advice Bureaux for this purpose
Painter, A.A. 138 L.G.R. 794   'Yet Another Consumer Agency?'   National
    Consumer Agency; is it necessary? Article also contains points on
    local enforcement of consumers' rights, consumer protection officers,
    trading standards officers etc.
— 138 L.G.R. 812   'A Local or National Service?'   Examines whether
    we should have a local or national consumer protection agency

Painter, A.A. 138 L.G.R. 837 'Who Prosecutes?' Article on prosecuting authority in consumer cases

— 138 L.G.R. 854 'In Support of Trade' Local authorities' support to consumerism by setting and enforcing weights and measures and quality standards (for food) etc.

— 138 L.G.R. 895 'The Art of Persuasion' Advertising and standards

— 138 L.G.R. 916 'The Unsolicited' Article on Unsolicited Goods and Services Act 1971

Rowlands, J. 138 L.G.R. 358 'Consumer and Safety' Covers ambit of Sale of Goods Act, consumer protection and local authority enforcement etc.

Thomas, W.H. LAG BULL. 190 'Consumer Rights: Gas and Electricity' Sets out in chart form the rights and duties of consumers and the gas and electricity authorities

1975

Anon. CRIM.L.R. 118 Case-note on Thomson Yellow Pages v. Pugh Unsolicited Goods and Services Act 1971 — directory entries

— 139 J.P. 66 'Consumer Protection Regulations' Brief note reporting new regulations in preparation

— 72 L.S.GAZ. 312 'Protection for readers on mail order advertisements' Practice note — new measures to protect consumers who send off advance payments in response to mail order ads

— 72 L.S.GAZ. 441 'Private sellers who aren't' Practice note — suggested new regulations to control advertisements by traders who do not disclose their business interest

Blackshaw, I.S. 125 N.L.J. 19 'Retailers' Liability — deterioration of food' Article on Tesco v. Roberts (1974), a decision dealing with the application and extent of Food and Drugs Act 1955 s. 2, and the scope of the 'warranty defence' under s. 115

Ervine, C. 125 N.L.J. 612 'The Director-General flexes his muscles' Article discussing procedure under Part II of the Fair Trading Act 1973 by which Director-General may remedy unfair practices

Lawson, R.G. 125 N.L.J. 568 'Some problems with the Unsolicited Goods and Services Act'

Painter, A. 139 L.G.R. 6 'The Year of the Consumer' Review of 1974 progress on consumer protection

— 139 L.G.R. 25 'Price Control' Importance of Prices Act 1974 in the fight against inflation

— 139 L.G.R. 44 'A voluntary code' Article advocating the voluntary agreement, or Code of Practice, as an important instrument of consumer protection

Painter, A. 139 L.G.R. 58 'Trial by Television' Article on the use of television in investigation of consumer problems

– 139 L.G.R. 80 'The Pinta' Consumer protection – control of milk quality

– 139 L.G.R. 96 'Advice for the consumer' Article on the need for consumer advice services, suggesting that efficient consumer advice can only flow from services supplied directly by county councils or CABx

– 139 L.G.R. 113 'Consumer education' Article on the need for a balanced approach to consumer education while maintaining consumer protection

– 139 L.G.R. 173 'The case for the specialist' The work of the modern consumer protection offices, and the need for a specialist approach to maintain high standards

– 139 L.G.R. 193 'Office without responsibility' Pessimistic discussion of the potential of the new National Consumer Council

– 139 L.G.R. 266 'A punishment to fit the crime' Article criticising the low penalties imposed in consumer protection cases

– 139 L.G.R. 342 'Labelling jungle' Article on the complexities of the law relating to food labelling

– 139 L.G.R. 580 'The consumer vote' Examination of the effects of EEC membership on the consumer

– 139 L.G.R. 447 'Consumer Council Confusion' Criticism of National Consumer Council proposals

– 139 L.G.R. 554 'Consumer protection statistics' Article on the problems affecting the collation of statistics for the consumer protection service, and reporting the first attempt to do so

– 139 L.G.R. 630 'Price information services' Discussion of Government proposals to encourage local authorities to develop pre-shopping information and price comparison services, and the possible serious consequences for the consumer protection services of non-participation by councils

– 139 L.G.R. 707 'Grand Advice' Consumer advice centres – criticism of government strategy

– 139 L.G.R. 766 'A Systolic Service' Note on Standard Weights and Measures Division of the Department of Prices and Consumer Protection

Whincup, M. 38 M.L.R. 660 'Reasonable fitness of cars' Discussion of law in Sale of Goods in light of recent cases and legislation including supply of Goods (Implied Terms) Act 1973, as amended by Consumer Credit Act 1974

(b) CONSUMER CREDIT

1971

Anon. 135 J.P. & L.G.R. 361   'The Crowther Report on Consumer Credit'
Comment and Summary of Report. (Cmnd. 4569)
–   68 L.S.GAZ. 355   'Crowther Report on Consumer Credit'   Editorial
–   115 S.J. 233   'Credit is due'   Comment on Crowther Report

1973

Anon. 117 S.J. 717   'Controlling Consumer Credit'   Note on White Paper
'Reform of Law on Consumer Credit'   Cmnd. 5427
–   117 S.J. 802   'Consumer Credit Bill'   Editorial
Feltham, J.D. 36 M.L.R. 174   'Fair Consumer Credit Laws: Report to the
Attorney General for the State of Victoria by a Committee of the Law
Council of Australia'   A comparison of Australian Committee's work
with the conclusions of the Crowther Report
Zeigel, J.S. 36 M.L.R. 479   'Recent Developments in Canadian Consumer
Credit Law'

1974

Adams, J.E. GUARDIAN/GAZETTE No. 105 p. 9   'The Consumer Credit
Act 1974'
Bennion, F.A.R. 118 S.J. 742   'Understanding the Consumer Credit Act
1974'
Lawson, R.G. 124 N.L.J. 839, 860, 880, 903, 941, 965, 989, 1013,
1023, 1064, 1088, 1109, 1136   Series of 13 articles on Consumer
Credit Act 1974
Painter, A.A. 138 L.G.R. 935   'Buying through Credit'   Consumer Credit
Act 1974
Prime, Terence 118 S.J. 799, 820   'Consumer Credit: A Guide'
Samuels, A. 71 L.S.GAZ. 29   'Reform of Law on Consumer Credit'

Anon. 72 L.S.GAZ. 68   'Consumer Credit Act 1974'   Practice note on
ss. 154, 155

– 72 L.S.GAZ. 419   'Consumer Credit Act'   Practice note – consul-
tation paper on application form for standard licences

Adams, J.E. 39 CONVEYANCER 94   'Mortgages and the Consumer Credit
Act 1974'   How the Act affects mortgages which constitute 'consumer
credit agreements'

Goode, R.M. C.L.J. 79   'The Consumer Credit Act 1974'   Detailed article
on background to Act, provisions, and assessment of its importance

Lawson, R.G. 125 N.L.J. 725   'Cheques, cheque cards and banking
practice'   How these are affected by the Consumer Credit Act 1974

McManus, J.J. 2 B.J.L.A.S. 66   'The Consumer Credit Act 1974'

Rogerson, A. 38 M.L.R. 435   'Consumer Credit Act 1975'   Commentary
on provisions of Act

Whitmore, J. 9 LAW TEACHER 1   'Consumer Credit Act 1974'   Long
article on the scope and purpose of the Act'

(c)   TRADE DESCRIPTIONS

1970

Anon. 134 J.P. & L.G.R. 121   'Misdescription'   Trade Descriptions Act
1968 and s. 14 on services, accommodation, amenities; applies
mainly to travel agents, brochures, etc.

Broome, A.J. 134 J.P. & L.G.R. 527   'Trade Descriptions Act 1968 – Third
Party Procedure'   Technical point on defences to Trade Descriptions
Act prosecutions, involving 3rd parties

O'Keefe, J. 120 N.L.J. 1176, 1196   'Absolute Offences and Defences'
in trade descriptions

1971

Anon. 136 L.G.R. 21   'Compensation Awarded Summarily for Fake Trade
Description'   Case from Croydon showing that Magistrates cannot
award compensation under s. 4 Forfeiture Act 1870 after convicting
a person of fake Trade Description; criticism of decision

Goudie, J. 135 J.P. & L.G.R. 235 'A Year of the Trade Descriptions Act 1968'

1972

Anon. 136 J.P. 666 'Trade Descriptions – 2 Controversial Decisions'
Comment on decision in Wycombe Marsh Garages v. Fowler (1972)
on s. 1 of Act, and Cottee v. Douglas Seaton (Red Cars) Ltd. (1972)
on s. 23

Cotter, B.G.H. 122 N.L.J. 755 'The case against oral Trade Descriptions'
Difficulties of prosectuion in cases of oral Trade Descriptions

Goudie, J. 136 L.G.R. 597 'Another Year of the Trade Descriptions Act'
Notable cases during the past year

1973

B.T.H. 137 J.P. 68 'Compensating the victims of false Trade Descriptions'
Parkes, W. 137 J.P. 744 'Trade Descriptions Act 1968 – Restrictions
imposed by judicial interpretation'
Samuels, Alec 117 S.J. 844 'Trade Descriptions Law in Action' Deals
with experience of Act and some suggested reforms

1974

Dobson, A.D. 8 LAW TEACHER 12 'Trade Descriptions Act 1968 –
Recent Decisions' 'Purpose of article is to see whether judicial interpretation has weakened or strengthened the effectiveness of the Act
as a principal piece of the legal armour which can protect the consumer'
White, A.R. 90 L.Q.R. 15 'Trade Description about the future' Case-
note on R. v. Sunair Holidays Ltd. (1973)

1975

Anon. CRIM.L.R. 53 Case-note on Whitehead v. Collett (1974) Trade
Descriptions Act 1968 s.11(2) – notice offering goods at price less
than in fact offered – immaterial that price not misleading per se

Anon. CRIM. L.R. 180 Case-note on Zawadsi v. Sleigh (1975) Trade descriptions — supply of vehicle with false odometer reading — liability of seller

— CRIM. L.R. 354 Case-note on Simmons v. Potter (1975) TDA 1968 s.24(1) — reliance on odometer reading no longer 'reasonable precautions' without disclaimer

— CRIM. L.R. 528 Case-note on Richards v. Westminster Motors (1975) Price stated not including VAT

— 139 J.P. 481 'Review of the Trade Descriptions Act' Summary of provisional conclusions of government review committee set up under Director-General of Fair Trading

— J.P.E.L. 471 Case-note on British Airways Board v. Taylor (1975) TDA 1968 s.14(1) — promise incapable of being 'false statement' within meaning of Act

— 139 L.G.R. 497 'What is a trade description?' Comment on Cadbury Ltd. v. Halliday (1975)

— 139 L.G.R. 633 'Reckless statements and the Trade Descriptions Act' Comment on British Airways v. Taylor (1975) and other authorities concerning defences to changes of making statements in breach of s.14(1) TDA 1968

Borrie, G. CRIM. L.R. 662 'A Review of The Trade Descriptions Act 1968'

Harper, T. 125 N.L.J. 811 'False statements on services' Note on findings of a review of operation of Trade Descriptions Act 1968, carried out under auspices of Office of Fair Trading

Lawson, R.G. 139 J.P. 223 'Statutory offences under the Trade Descriptions Act'

— 139 J.P. 716 'Statutory defences under the Trade Descriptions Act' Considers recent cases and the consultative document

— 125 N.L.J. 948, . . . 'The Consultative Document: some comments and proposals — I On Trade Descriptions Act 1968

Milner, A. 38 M.L.R. 694 'The Rape of the Trade Descriptions Act' Note on British Airways v. Taylor (1975)

Newsome, E.L. 125 N.L.J. 225 'Disclaimers, Understandings and the Doctrine of Caveat Emptor' Implications of decision in Norman v. Bennett on enforcement of TDA 1968 and 1972

— 125 N.L.J. 1213 'Mileometers — The Obvious Protection' Article on impact of Trade Descriptions Act on second hand car sales

Roberts, J.L. 139 J.P. 88 'Unusual Trade Descriptions' Reports of prosecutions under TDA 1968

(d)   SMALL CLAIMS

1970

Anon. L.S.GAZ. 587   'A Small Claims Court?'   Article based on an assess-
       ment and analysis of the Consumer Council's 'Justice Out Of Reach'
–   120 N.L.J. 285   'Small Claims: A New Approach'   Review of costs
       of present procedure, and a conference held by Consumer Council
       on implications of this position and its possible remedies
–   120 N.L.J. 765   'Justice Out Of Reach'   Editorial
–   120 N.L.J. 783   'A Small Claims Court'   Summary of Consumer
       Council proposals
–   120 N.L.J. 827   'Small Claims and Legal Representation'   Comment
       on small claims courts
–   114 S.J. 625   'Justice Out Of Reach'   Comment on Consumer
       Council Report
Grayson, E. 120 N.L.J. 824   'Comment: The Reach of Justice'   Examines
       role of county court jurisdiction, High Court jurisdiction, purpose
       and function of magistrates' civil jurisdiction etc. raised by Justice
       Report

1971

Anon. 135 J.P. & L.G.R. 787   'Small Claims and County Court'   Note on
       Lord Hailsham's unfavourable reaction to pressure for small claims
       court as advocated in 'Justice Out Of Reach'
–   68 L.S.GAZ. 299   'Small Claims Court'   The Manchester court;
       editorial comment
–   121 N.L.J. 3   'Small Claims and Legal Representation'   Editorial
       on Lord Chancellor's reaction to 'Justice Out Of Reach'
–   121 N.L.J. 50   'Representation Or Not – And The Price'   A re-
       joinder to editorial (above) emphasising cost of legal representation
       in small claims area
–   121 N.L.J. 95   'The Small Claims Courts Bill'   Details and ex-
       amination of Michael Meacher M.P.'s private member's bill on small
       claims court
–   121 N.L.J. 229   'Problems of Small Claims Courts'   Examination
       of Consumer Council's proposal and activities of lawyers in the pro-
       posed set-up
–   121 N.L.J. 607   'Small Claims – Manchester Arbitration Scheme'
       Comment

Anon. 121 N.L.J. 965 'Dilemmas Of The Small Claim' Account of Lord
    Hailsham's comments on costs of litigation in such claims and review
    of costs
–   115 S.J. 46 'The Small Debts Problem' Deals with county courts'
    uneconomic procedures, proposals of Consumer Council, and litigants
    in person
–   115 S.J. 118 'Disputes Bigger Than Claims' Comment on pro-
    posals to bar lawyers from small claims procedure
Howard-Luck, C.A. 135 J.P. & L.G.R. 862 'Bring Justice Within Reach'
    Deals with 'Justice Out Of Reach', events subsequent to Report,
    implementation of recommendations and other details

1972

Anon. 136 J.P. 535 'Small Claims' Comment on Young Solicitors' Group
    of the Law Society's views on this topic
–   LAG BULL. 10 'The Manchester Arbitration Scheme' Description
    of scheme, and its operation in first nine months
–   122 N.L.J. 118 'Small Claims and Pre-Trial Review' Editorial
    on objectives and methods of pre-trial procedure under new county
    court rules
–   116 S.J. 750 'Legal Aid Philosophy' Case for legal aid to all in
    small claims cases (and see Legal Aid)
Foster, K. 116 S.J. 502 'The Manchester Arbitration Scheme' Deals with
    philosophy behind scheme, procedure, hearings and costs
Ison, T.G. 35 M.L.R. 18 'Small Claims' An examination of the present
    county court system and possibilities for reform

1973

Anon. 137 J.P. 154 'Small Claims Courts' Hailsham's views on small
    claims courts reported on his opening of Wandsworth County Court
–   137 J.P. 241 'Consumer Courts' and 'Advice Centres' Two
    editorials dealing with Government's thinking on arbitration scheme
    administered through county courts, and on advice centres linked to
    office of Fair Trading (see also Consumer Protection: General)
–   137 J.P. 516 'Small Claims Arbitration' Note on new county court
    rules widening procedure for dealing with small claims
–   70 L.S.GAZ. 1783 'Small Claims Court For Westminster' Note
    contains views of Robert Egerton, the organiser

Anon.   70 L.S.GAZ. 2226   'Arbitration Service in County Court — New Facilities for Dealing with Small Claims'   Practice note

—   70 L.S.GAZ. 2285   'Arbitration — The Manchester Experiment' Editorial

—   70 L.S.GAZ. 2458   'Westminster Law Society opens a Small Claims Court'

—   LAG BULL. 27   'We Still Need A Small Claims System'   Article on Manchester Arbitration Scheme, and evidence which it provides of unmet need for this type of scheme. Concludes that solution is small claims system should operate in county court system

—   LAG BULL. 186   'At Least A Half Hog From The Lord Chancellor' A comparison between the new county court small claims arbitration scheme and the Manchester Arbitration Scheme

—   LAG BULL. 203   'Small Claims Arbitration — New County Court Rules'   Practical details

—   123 N.L.J. 142   'Small Claims — Howe Now'   Views of Sir G. Howe on nature of consumer advice services and his criticisms of types of case coming before available institutions. N.L.J. criticises him for his apparent abandonment of the small claims court idea

—   123 N.L.J. 265   'Small Claims Courts — The Lord Chancellor Elucidates'   Details of the Lord Chancellor's views on small claims courts and his wish to see county courts taking prominence in this area. Criticism of his statement by N.L.J.

—   123 N.L.J. 383   'Small Claims — Gathering The Evidence'   City of Westminster Law Society opened new small claims court.   Article focuses on this and problems and limitations placed on such courts; presses Government for final decision on question

—   123 N.L.J. 777   'Small Claims Procedure'   Comment on publication of the small claims procedure to be established in the county court system; some criticism of its provisions for privacy in hearings and monetary limits

—   123 N.L.J. 785   'New Facilities For Dealing With Small Claims — Arbitration Service in the County Court'   Details of S.I. 1973/1412 amending county court rules to introduce new facilities

—   123 N.L.J. 898   'How To Sue'   A comment on the opening of Westminster Small Claims Court and Consumers Association guide 'How to Sue In The County Court'

—   113 S.J. 154   'Small Claims In The Judicial System'   Suggests a small claims scheme grafted onto county courts

Egerton, R.   70 L.S.GAZ. 2276   'Arbitration in County Courts'

Foster, K. LAG BULL. 190   'The Manchester Arbitration Scheme – An
Interim Report'   Analysis of the Manchester Scheme

1974

Anon. 118 S.J. 43   'Arbitration In County Courts'
Egerton, R. 71 L.S.GAZ. 427   'The Westminster Small Claims Court'
Survey of its work; implicaton that its existence is little known

1975

Anon. 125 N.L.J. 881   'County Court Arbitrations' Editorial on latest
statistics on small claims arbitration in county courts
–   125 N.L.J. 1182   'Small Claims – the case for survival' Editorial
on the current state of experiments with procedures in dealing with small
claims
Foster, K. 2 B.J.L.A.S. 75   'Problems with small claims' Questioning
whether legal reform, leading to small claims system , is the best solution to consumer problems, and results of research into the Manchester
scheme
Harper, T. 125 N.L.J. 735   'Small Claims' Note on Which? investigation of
county court small claims procedures
Sherwin, M. LAG BULL. 65   'The Westminster Small Claims Court'

(e)   DEBT COLLECTION

1970

Anon. 120 N.L.J. 807   'Bad Debts – The Other Side To Harassment'
Editorial on survey carried out by Tracing Services Group, a company
specialising in tracing bad debtors, into evasion of debts
Black, A. 67 L.S.GAZ. 42   ' . . . The Skirts Of The Penniless Widows'
Article on the Report of the Committee on the Enforcement of
Judgment Debts (Cmnd. 3909)
Borrie, G. & Pyke, J. 120 N.L.J. 564   'Administration of Justice Act 1970 –
Enforcement of Debts'
–   120 N.L.J. 588   'The Administration of Justice Act 1970 – Harass-
ment of Debtors'

Anon. 135 J.P. & L.G.R. 671 'Attachment' Note on Attachment of Earnings Act 1971

— 135 J.P. & L.G.R. 683 'Attachment' Comment on the Act

Chambers, G.S. 135 J.P. & L.G.R. 814 'Attachment and Means Inquiries' Deals with points of practice and procedure under Attachment of Earnings Act, 1971

Poole, F.T. LAW GUARDIAN No. 71 p. 17 'Dealing With Debt' A review of the reasoning of the Payne Committee that led to restriction of imprisonment for debt, and to attachment of earnings instead — Administration of Justice Act, 1970

Glasser, C. 34 M.L.R. 61 'Administration of Justice Act 1970: Enforcement of Debt Provisions' The Act's provisions following the recommendations of the Payne Committee

1972

Anon. 1 I.L.J. 31 'Attachment of Earnings Act 1971' Comment

1974

Oliver, D. LAG BULL. 238 'Administration Orders, A Useful Procedure For Debtors' Article about administration orders in the county courts, as a means by which a debtor can pay off creditors fairly, without threat of harassment

1975

Samuels, A. 72 L.S.GAZ. 727 'Enforcement of Debts' Examination of ways of recovering debts

(a)   TRIBUNALS AND INQUIRIES

1970

Anon. 120 N.L.J. 847 'Legal Representation and Tribunals' (Editorial)
−   120 N.L.J. 845   'The Tribunal Explosion' 11th Annual Report
          of Council on Tribunals on proliferation of tribunals; comment on
          Report
Samuels, A. 114 S.J. 4 'Legal Aid and Rent Control Tribunals' Points
          out failure to make provision for legal aid before rent tribunals and
          need to do so. (And see LEGAL AID)
Yardley, D.C.M. 114 S.J. 24 'Legal Aid and Rent Control Tribunals:
          A Reply' Reply to Alec Samuels

1971

Samuels, A. 121 N.L.J. 397 'Administrative Tribunals: The Future'
          Some statistics on tribunals in U.K. and future of tribunals

1972

Anon. 122 N.L.J. 505 'Tribunals and Natural Justice' Editorial on what
          should be the prime criteria for tribunals: cheapness, accessibility,
          expedition, freedom from technicality or dispensation of justice
          Is latter being lost for sake of former?
−   122 N.L.J. 507 'Trial by Tribunal − Onus of Proof' Editorial
          commenting on tribunal handling of co-habitation cases and the onus
          of proof involved
−   122 N.L.J. 1073 'Clamour Unheard' Editorial on the 1972 report
          of Council on Tribunals which also considers demands for reform in
          this area and extension to it of legal aid
−   136 L.G.R. 202   'The Council on Tribunals Dislikes Fair Rent
          Procedure' Short note on Council's 1970-71 Report. Notes
          Council's objections to Rent Scrutiny Committees under Housing
          Finance Bill, Part V, not accepted

Alder, J.E. PUB.L. 278 'Representation Before Tribunals' Article concerning the right of representation before tribunals

Field, F. 122 N.L.J. 1007 'Tribunals: Poor People's Courts' Article on supplementary benefits appeals tribunals, noting the effect of their decisions on 5 million poor people who are more or less dependent on welfare payments

Rose, H. 122 N.L.J. 774, 786 'Tribunals: General Practice Complaints — Case for a Patients' Advocate' Projected remedies for complaints in medical system

1973

Anon. 137 J.P. 431 'Legal Aid Before Tribunals'

— 70 L.S.GAZ. 2054 'Legal Aid in Tribunals' Note that Lord Chancellor's Legal Aid Advisory Committee is reviewing this subject

— 137 L.G.R. 125 'Tribunals' A note dealing with the latest Report of the Council on Tribunals — with emphasis on findings concerning local government

— 123 N.L.J. 649 'Legal Aid in Tribunals' Article arguing for extension of legal aid to tribunals

— 117 S.J. 921 'Legal Aid Before Tribunals' Arguments for and against this idea

Archer, P. GUARDIAN/GAZETTE No. 89, p. 19 'Tribunals Galore' Mainly concentrates on working of welfare tribunals; statistics; representation

O'Brien, R.J. 123 N.L.J. 974 'Award of Costs at Inquiries' Review of statutory power to make orders as to costs in local inquiries, particularly compulsory purchase and planning inquiries

Pollock, S. 70 L.S.GAZ. 1250 'A Review of the Annual Report of the Council on Tribunals'

1974

Anon. LAG BULL. 27 'Tribunal Representation: LAG Calls for a National Network' LAG's representation to the Lord Chancellor's Advisory Committee

— 71 L.S.GAZ. 53 'Tribunal or Court' Review of 'Tribunals — A Social Court?' by Fulbrook, Brooke and Archer. Gives quick and short review of some major criticism of tribunal appeal system, particularly in DHSS and SBC area

Anon.   71 L.S.GAZ. 338   'Representation Before Tribunals'   Comment on
Memorandum of Council of Law Society to Lord Chancellor's Advisory
Committee on this point.   Says there is need to increase representation,
but at same time restrict spending

–   71 L.S.GAZ. 450   'Tribunal Chaos'   Editorial on Annual Report
(72-73) of Council on Tribunals; linked to comments in 'Tribunals –
A Social Court?' (See also 138 L.G.R. 376)

–   124 N.L.J. 257   'Hope For Legal Aid'   Comment on Reports of
Law Society and the Lord Chancellor's Advisory Committee on Legal
Aid for 1972-73 (H.C.–1).   Notes the major findings of Report as the
lack of legal aid to poor (in particular) and others in tribunal cases
(and see LEGAL AID)

–   124 N.L.J. 398   'Legal Aid Special Number'   Various proposals
(LAG, Justice, Paddington, NCCL, Law Society) on legal aid in
tribunals

Brooke, R. 124 N.L.J. 100   'Tribunals – A Social Court?'   A precis version
of Brooke, Archer and Fulbrooke, 'Tribunals – A Social Court'
Concentration on social security tribunals – statistics – proliferation
of tribunals.   Recommendation of a 'social court' in place of tribunal
system.   This intended to check proliferation of tribunals

Street, H.   LAG BULL. 128   'Tribunals: Two New Publications'   Review
of 'Administrative Tribunals', Wraith and Hutcheson, and 'Tribunals:
A Social Court?' by Fulbrook, Brooke and Archer

1975

Anon.   J.P.E.L. 314   'Current Topics'   Note on council on Tribunals'
Annual Report

–   125 N.L.J. 345   'Light on Tribunals'   Editorial on report on operation of the national insurance appeals tribunal system

–   125 N.L.J. 397   'Watching over Tribunals'   Editorial on Council
on Tribunals' Annual Report 1973/74

–   125 N.L.J. 565   'Tribunals and individual rights'   Editorial on
CPAG report by Ruth Lister, Welfare in Action – 'an indictment of
the Council on Tribunals for its treatment of complaints about SBATs'

Brown, I.   139 L.G.R. 42   'Public Enquiries and Public Confidence'   Article
emphasising the need to retain public confidence if the public local
enquiry is to continue as a useful instrument

Harper, T.   125 N.L.J. 447   'Welfare Appeals'   Note on The Appellant and
his Case by Julian Fulbrook (CPAG) – 'an important contribution to

the growing literature on the operation of welfare tribunals'

Harper, T. 125 N.L.J. 883 'Irresponsible response' Note on reply from Chairman of Council on Tribunals to CPAG criticisms of Council in Welfare in Action (see above)

Turner, S. 32 POVERTY 29 'The Trade Union Role in Tribunals' Report of research done in connection with Professor K. Bell's research on National Insurance and Supplementary Benefits Appeal Tribunals

(b) PUBLIC PARTICIPATION

1972

Anon. 69 L.S.GAZ. 921 'Town Planning and Participation' Editorial comment on Sir D. Heap's inaugural address on this topic

Heap, Sir Desmond J.P.L. 683 'Sir Desmond Heap on Public Participation in the Planning Process'

Samuels, A. J.P.L. 427 'Participation in the Application for Planning Permission'

1973

Bigham, A. J.P.E.L. 6 'The Shaping of Our Environment: Problems of Participation'

Pope, A.S. J.P.E.L. 159 'South Essex: A Planning Choice. An Exercise in Public Participation'

1974

Anon. 13 COMMUNITY ACTION 13 'Public Inquiries' Action Report prepared by Shelter Community Action Team — what is a public inquiry, how to succeed at them, arguments available for particular CPOs

 — 14 COMMUNITY ACTION 11 — 'Community Action and the Police'

    15 — 11

    16 — 22

Three-part report on the laws which affect direct action by tenants and community groups and the role of the police in attempting to control it — public meetings, marches and demonstrations, evictions, occupations, rent strikes, picketing, etc.

Valerian, A. 125 N.L.J. 176 'Public participation in planning – the practice
so far' Article on West Midlands experience of public participation
in planning
– 125 N.L.J. 804 'Structure plans – the examination in public'
Article on examination in public, which replaced traditional public
inquiry by virtue of Town & Country Planning (Amendment) Act 1972

(c) OMBUDSMEN

1970

Anon. LAW GUARDIAN No. 57 p. 1 'Maladministration' Maladministra-
tion at the DHSS in relation to a delay in industrial injuries benefit
case
– 114 S.J. 234 'Tip of the Iceberg' Comment on 2nd Report of
PCA; criticises 'straightjacket' imposed on his work by the Parlia-
mentary Commissioner Act 1967
Drake, C.D. 48 PUBLIC ADMINISTRATION 179 'Ombudsmen for Local
Government'
Foulkes, D. JOURNAL OF BUSINESS LAW 266 'The PCA and Business
Law'

1971

Foulkes, D. 34 M.L.R. 377 'The Discretionary Provisions of the Parliamentary Commissioner Act 1967' Article considers the Commissioner's treatment of those discretionary provisions relating to his
jurisdiction
Sullivan, J.M. J.P.L. 7 and 80 'Planning and the Parliamentary Commissioner' Analysis of Ombudsman's role in planning process and use
made of him on planning cases up to 1970
Jackson, P. PUB.L. 39 'The Work of the PCA'

1972

Anon. J.P.L. 295 Editorial note on announcement of setting up of complaints system for local government

Benson, G.N. 116 S.J. 347 'The Parliamentary Commissioner' Report on Ombudsman's Report 1971

Cohen, L.H. PUB.L. 204 'The Parliamentary Commissioner for Administration and the M.P. Filter'

Elcock, H.J. 50 PUBLIC ADMINISTRATION 87 'Opportunity for Ombudsman: The Norther Ireland Commissioner for Complaints'

Gregory, R. and Alexander, A. 50 PUBLIC ADMINISTRATION 313 'Our Parliamentary Ombudsman'

1973

Anon. 137 L.G.R. 866 'Complaints About Maladministration' The scheme of Ombudsman conceived for local government

Burke, R. 137 L.G.R. 887 'Local Complaints' Article dealing with proposed local 'ombudsman' scheme

Marshall, G. PUB.L. 32 'Maladministration' An examination of what the term 'maladministration' actually means in Parliamentary Commissioner 1967 Act in the light of cases considered under it

1974

Anon. 138 L.G.R. 299 'Parts III and IV of the Local Government Act, 1972 – I' Substantially deals with the role of the local complaints commissioners – ombudsmen

– 138 L.G.R. 314 'Investigating Maladministration in Local Government' Note on Local Government Act 1974, which set up local ombudsman and detailed working of system vis-a-vis local authorities

Garner, J.F. 37 M.L.R. 473 Review of 'Maladministration and its Remedies' by K.C. Wheare

– 118 S.J. 155 'The Commissions for Local Administration' Local Government Act, 1974, Part III establishing local government commissioners (or 'ombudsmen'). Article deals with jurisdiction, procedure, etc.

1975

(Non-select reports of local government ombudsman now available monthly in J.P.E.L., p.543 ff.)

Brown, I. 139 L.G.R. 459 'Ombundsmen one and all' Article on the work of the Commission of Local Administration
Harper, T. 125 N.L.J. 543 'Local Ombudsman' Note on Your Local Ombudsman by Commission for Local Government Administration in England
Street, H. 39 CONVEYANCER 327 'The Parliamentary Commissioner: The Champion of Landowners with a grievance against Central Government'

(d)   JUDICIAL CONTROL OF THE ADMINISTRATION

(Articles on Administrative Law problems of particular interest to welfare lawyers)

1970

Akehurst, M. 33 M.L.R. 154 'Statements of Reasons for Judicial and Administrative Decisions' Article which argues that there is no common law rule that statement of reasons is necessary
Garner, J.F. 114 S.J. 816 and 837 'Means of Review of Planning Procedures'
Whitmore, H. 33 M.L.R. 481 'The Role of the Lawyer in Administrative Justice' Discusses role of lawyers in administration. Puts forward a plea for increased concern with this in teaching etc.

1971

Anon. 121 N.L.J. 537 'Administrative Decision-Making' Editorial on Justice Report on 'Administration Under Law' which concludes that more effective safeguards are required against administrative bureaucracy (and see OMBUDSMEN)
Garner, J.F. 135 J.P. & L.G.R. 486 'Administration Under Law' Summary of Justice Report 'Administration'

Zellick, G. 121 N.L.J. 390 'The Right to Legal Representation'
Discussion of this in light of Pett v. Greyhound Racing (1969) and
Enderby Town v. F.A. (1971) Contains bibliography of other articles
on representation, natural justice etc.

1972

Lawton, D.A. LAW GUARDIAN No. 79 p.23 'Lawful Power and the
Citizen'
Trice, J.E. J.P.L. 418 'Administrative Law Reform: A Survey'
Williams, E.A. LAW GUARDIAN No. 81 p.23 'The Citizen and Lawful
Power' Discussion of problems raised by A. Douglas Lawton in
Law Guardian No. 79, p.23, and discussion of the problems relating
to private rights and public works

1973

Bentil, J.K. PUB.L. 80 'Disregarding the Finality of a Determination by
Statutory Authorities and the Order of Certiorari' Case note on
Jones v. Secretary of State for Social Services (1972) Discusses
what constitutes an 'error of law' on part of an administrative tribunal so that certiorari will issue to quash decision
Birtles, B. LAG BULL. 273 'Remedies in Administrative Law' Discussion
of the potential for poverty lawyers of prohibition, certiorari,
mandamus and the judicial declaration, particularly against local
authorities and as a method of appeal from tribunals. (Injunctions
not discussed)
Ganz, G. PUB.L. 84 'Compensation for Negligent Administrative Action'
Jowell, J. PUB.L. 178 'The Legal Control of Administrative Discretion'
The article examines the extent to which legal techniques should
be invoked to control administrative discretion; the discussion
focuses attention on techniques of control at the point of decision
and concentrates on the area of welfare rights and land-use planning

1974

Dickens, R.M. LAG BULL. 273 'Public Interest Litigation – Relator and
Representative Action' The article describes the limited procedures
available for individuals or groups who wish to take legal proceedings
to compel public bodies to observe the law

Jacob, J. PUB.L. 25 'Some Reflections on Governmental Secrecy'
Discusses how officialdom handles other people's secrets; the article
is concerned particularly with the role of governmental secrecy vis-a-vis
community pressure groups, environmental groups, etc.
Scarman, Sir L. LAG BULL. 262 'Administrative Law and the Legal Profession' The text of an address given in 1969 on the role of the legal
profession in assisting people whose livelihoods are reviewed and/or
jeopardised by administrative action or decision
Williams, D.W. 138 L.G.R. 833 'Natural Justice and Local Authorities'

1975

Hodge, H. LAG BULL. 86 'The long retreat' Comment on implication
of Lord Denning's judgment in R v. Preston SBAT, ex p Moore
for claimants' rights under the law
—   125 N.L.J. 595 'Judicial Withdrawal' Article on CA decisions in
SB cases: ex p Moore
Markson, H.E. 119 S.J. 110 'Rent Tribunals: Mandamus and Certiorari'
Article on effect of R v. Kensington & Chelsea Rent Tribunal, ex p
MacFarlane (1974) — a further illustration of the circumstances in
which courts may order mandamus directed to a rent tribunal
Seepersad, C.P. PUB.L. 242 'Fairness and Andi Alteram Partem' General
discussion of the extent to which the courts will impose standards of
fairness on administrative bodies
Street, H. LAG BULL 118 'Judicial Review Refused' Importance of CA
decision in R. v. Preston SBAT, ex p Moore, especially on the
relationship between the ordinary courts and SBATs

(e)   COMPLAINTS AGAINST LAWYERS

1970

Anon. 67 L.S.GAZ. 229 'Justice Report on Complaints Against Lawyers'
Editorial comment
—   120 N.L.J. 261 'The Complaint and the Cure' Editorial on Law
Society Council's statement on complaints against solicitors
—   120 N.L.J. 280 'Complaints Against Lawyers' A lengthy review
of the complaints report given by Justice. Includes Justice's proposed
investigation procedure, and a statement on complaints by Law

119

Society

Garrett, G. 120 N.L.J. 345 'Not Only . . . But Also' Shorter note on Justice Report on complaints against lawyers

Miller, G. 33 M.L.R. 542 'Justice Report on Complaints Against Lawyers' A discussion

1971

Garrett, G.E. LAW GUARDIAN No. 66 p.17 'Complaints Against Lawyers' A further comment, by one of its authors, on the Justice Report on complaints against lawyers

1974

Hewetson, C. 71 L.S.GAZ. 164 'Professional Purposes – 1. Complaints' Work of Professional Purposes Committee of Law Society's Council – deals with complaints

1975

Anon. 125 N.L.J. 154 'Complaints against solicitors' Appointment of lay observer under Solicitors Act 1957 s.28A to examine written allegations against solicitors

SECTION B

BOOKS

(All books are published in London, England,
unless otherwise indicated)

I   THE LEGAL SYSTEM AND THE POOR

(See Westergaard, pp. l6, 32-4, and 110-121; Blackstone, Ch.VII, Ch.XII, pp. 102-3, 123-130)

(a)   LEGAL SERVICES

Abel-Smith, B., Zander, M. and Brooke, R., LEGAL PROBLEMS AND THE CITIZEN, Heinemann, 1973

American Bar Association, Project to Assist Interested Law Firms in Pro Bono Publico Programs THE LAWYER AS A VOLUNTEER   Chicago: American Bar Association, 1972

Anon. LEGAL REPRESENTATION OF THE POOR: THE NEW YORK CITY EXPERIENCE N.Y: Practising Law Institute, 1970

Berney, A.L., Goldberg, J., Dooley, J.A., and Carroil, D.W.   LEGAL PROBLEMS OF THE POOR   Boston: Little, Brown, 1975

Bond, N. and Zara, R., CDP LEGAL AND INCOME RIGHTS PROGRAMME: CASEWORK CAMPAIGNS AND ADULT EDUCATION   Coventry: Community Development Project, 1975

Brasnett, M., THE STORY OF THE CITIZENS' ADVICE BUREAUX, National Council for Social Service, 1964

Bridges, L., Sufrin, B., Whetton, J. & White, R., LEGAL SERVICES IN BIRMINGHAM   Birmingham: Institute of Judicial Administration, 1975

British Columbia, Delivery of Legal Services Project   SYSTMES OF DEL-IVERY Vancouver: Justice Development Commission, 1974

Brooke, R., INFORMATION AND ADVICE SERVICES   G. Bell & Sons, 1972

Brooke, R., Field, F., Townsend, P., A POLICY TO ESTABLISH THE LEGAL RIGHTS OF LOW INCOME FAMILIES: LEGAL AID AND ADVICE C.P.A.G., 1969

Bryant, R. and Bradshaw, J., WELFARE RIGHTS AND SOCIAL ACTION: THE YORK EXPERIMENT C.P.A.G., 1970

Bull, D., ACTION FOR WELFARE RIGHTS   Fabian Society, 1970

Carlin, J.E., Howard, J. and Messinger, S.L. CIVIL JUSTICE AND THE POOR N.Y: Russell Sage Foundation, 1967

Cass, M. and Sackville, R. LEGAL NEEDS OF THE POOR   Canberra: Australian Govt. Print. Serv., 1975

Christensen, B.F. LAWYERS FOR PEOPLE OF MODERATE MEANS: SOME PROBLEMS OF AVAILABILITY   Chicago: American Bar Foundation, 1970

Committee on Legal Services to the Poor in the Developing Countries LEGAL AID AND WORLD POVERTY New York: Praeger, 1974

Curran, B.A. and Spalding, F.O. THE LEGAL NEEDS OF THE PUBLIC
    Chicago: American Bar Association, 1974
Dell, S. SILENT IN COURT Bell, 1971
Dodyk , P.M. (ed) and others CASES AND MATERIALS ON LAW AND
    POVERTY St. Paul, Minn: West Pub. Co., 1969
Fisher, K.P. FRANCHISING JUSTICE Chicago: American Bar Foundation,
    1971
Friedland, M.L. ACCESS TO THE LAW: A STUDY Toronto: Carswell/
    Methuen, 1975
Getty, G.W., and Presley, J. PUBLIC DEFENDER New York: Grosset &
    Dunlop, 1974
Goldman, M.C. THE PUBLIC DEFENDER (1917 ed) New York: Arno
    Press, 1974
Hodge, H., LEGAL RIGHTS Arrow, 1974
Johnson, E. JUSTICE AND REFORM N.Y: Russell Sage Foundation, 1974
Law Society (England & Wales), Young Solicitors Group TOMORROW'S
    LAWYERS Law Society, 1971
Legal Action Group LEGAL ADVICE CENTRES – AN EXPLOSION? LAG,
    1972
Legal Action Group LEGAL SERVICES FOR THE FUTURE LAG, 1974
Leissner, A. FAMILY ADVICE SERVICES Longmans, 1967
Lynes, T. WELFARE RIGHTS Fabian Society, 1970
Marks, F.R. THE SHREVEPORT PLAN: AN EXPERIMENT IN THE DEL–
    IVERY OF LEGAL SERVICES Chicago: American Bar Foundation,
    1974
McCarthy, B.A. LEGAL SERVICES TO THE POOR: A SELECTIVE BIBLI–
    OGRAPHY Sacramento, Calif: California State Library, Law
    Library, 1970
McCarthy, C.P. THE CONSEQUENCES OF LEGAL ADVOCACY: OEO'S
    LAWYERS AND THE POOR (Thesis: University of California,
    Berkeley) Ann Arbor, Mich: University Microfilms, 1974
Morris, P., White, R., & Lewis, P. SOCIAL NEEDS AND LEGAL ACTION
    Martin Robertson, 1973
Parker, F.J. THE LAW AND THE POOR Mary Knoll, N.Y: Orbis Books,
    1973
Partington, M.   RECENT DEVELOPMENTS IN LEGAL SERVICES FOR
    THE POOR: SOME REFLECTIONS ON EXPERIENCE IN COVEN–
    TRY Coventry: Community Development Project, 1975
Pfennigstorf, W.   LEGAL EXPENSE INSURANCE: THE EUROPEAN EX–
    PERIENCE Chicago: American Bar Foundation, 1975
Rockwell, R.C.   A STUDY OF LAW AND THE POOR IN CAMBRIDGE
    MASS. Cambridge, Mass: Community Legal Assistance Office, 1968
Rosenthal, D.E. VOLUNTEER ATTORNEYS AND LEGAL SERVICES FOR

THE POOR   New York: Russell Sage Foundation, 1971

Sackville, R.   LAW AND POVERTY IN AUSTRALIA   Canberra: Australian
Govt. Print Serv., 1976

Silverstein, L.   DEFENSE OF THE POOR IN AMERICAN STATE COURTS;
A FIELD STUDY & REPORT   Chicago: American Bar Foundation,
1965

Smith, R.H.   JUSTICE AND THE POOR   New York: Carnegie Foundation
for the Advancement of Teaching, 1919

Smith, S.C.   PUBLIC LEGAL SERVICE: SELECTED RECENT WRITINGS
New Haven: Yale Law Library, May, 1969

Society of Conservative Lawyers,   ROUGH JUSTICE   Conservative Political
Centre, 1968

Society of Labour Lawyers   JUSTICE FOR ALL   Fabian Society, 1968

Stumpf, H.P.   COMMUNITY POLITICS AND LEGAL SERVICES   Beverley
Hills, Calif: Sage Publications, 1975

Taman, L.   THE LEGAL SERVICES CONTROVERSY   Ottawa: National
Council of Welfare, 1971

U.S., Congress, House, Committee on Education and Labor, Subcommittee
on Equal Opportunities   ESTABLISHMENT OF A LEGAL SER—
VICES CORPORATION   Washington: U.S. Govt. Print Off., 1973

(b)   LEGAL AID

Borrie, G.J. and Varcoe, J.R.   LEGAL AID IN CRIMINAL PROCEEDINGS —
A REGIONAL SURVEY   Birmingham: Institute of Judicial Administration, 1973

Brakel, S.J.   JUDICARE: PUBLIC FUNDS, PRIVATE LAWYERS, AND
POOR PEOPLE   Chicago: American Bar Foundation, 1974

Cappelletti, M., Gordley', J. and Johnson, E.   TOWARD EQUAL JUSTICE
A COMPARATIVE STUDY OF LEGAL AID IN MODERN
SOCIETIES   Milan: Guiffre, Dobbs Ferry, New York: Oceana,
1975

Christensen, B.R.   LAWYERS FOR PEOPLE OF MODERATE MEANS
Chicago: American Bar Foundation, 1970

Egerton, R.   LEGAL AID   Oxford University Press, 1945

Fea, G.B.   LEGAL AID IN NEW ZEALAND   Wellington, N.Z.: Butterworths, 1975

Graham-Green, G.J.   CRIMINAL COSTS INCLUDING LEGAL AID   Butterworths, 1965

G.B. Committee on Legal Advice in England and Wales, REPORT (Chairman:
Lord Rushcliffe) (Cmd ⊦. 6641) HMSO, 1945

G.B. Departmental Committee on Legal Aid in Criminal Proceedings REPORT
(Chairman: Mr. Justice Widgery) (Cmnd. 2934) HMSO, 1966

G.B., Lord Chancellor's Advisory Committee on Legal Aid, ANNUAL RE-
    PORTS ON LEGAL AID   Published with those of the Law Society
    HMSO, 1950–date
G.B., Lord Chancellor's Advisory Committee   REPORT (Cmnd. 918) HMSO,
    1959
G.B., Lord Chancellor's Advisory Committee   REPORT (Cmnd. 962) HMSO,
    1960
G.B., Lord Chancellor's Advisory Committee on Legal Aid   REPORT ON THE
    BETTER PROVISION OF LEGAL ADVICE AND ASSISTANCE
    (Cmnd. 4249) HMSO, 1970
G.B. Parliament Estimates Committee   FOURTH REPORT ON LEGAL AID
    (H.C. 209/1955-56) HMSO, 1956
G.B. Supplementary Benefits Commission   HANDBOOK (4th ed, ch.XV)
    HMSO, 1974
G.B. Government White Paper   LEGAL AID AND ADVICE BILL
    (Cmd . 7563) HMSO, 1948
G.B. Working Party on Legal Aid in Criminal Proceedings   FIRST REPORT
    HMSO, 1962
G.B. Working Party on Legal Aid in Criminal Proceedings   FINAL REPORT
    HMSO, 1963
Gurney-Champion, F.C.G. JUSTICE AND THE POOR IN ENGLAND
    Routledge, 1926
Haldane Society   THE LAW AND RECONSTRUCTION   Haldane Society,
    1942
Harris, B. & Rickard, R. LEGAL AID AND ADVICE   Chichester: Barry
    Rose, 1975
Law Society ANNUAL REPORTS ON LEGAL AID   Published with Lord
    Chancellor's Advisory Committee on Legal Aid HMSO, 1950–date
Law Society LEGAL AID HANDBOOK (3rd ed) HMSO, 1966 (loose-
    leaf)
Law Society   MEMORANDUM ON LEGAL ADVICE AND ASSISTANCE
    Law Society, 1968
Law Society SECOND MEMORANDUM ON LEGAL ADVICE AND ASSIS-
    TANCE Law Society, 1969
Law Society REPORT OF THE SPECIAL COMMITTEE OF THE LAW
    SOCIETY ON LEGAL AID AND ADVICE Law Society, 1946
Law Society of Northern Ireland   ANNUAL REPORTS ON LEGAL AID
    Belfast: HMSO, 1966–date
Law Society of Scotland REPORT ON LEGAL AID SCHEME   Edinburgh,
    HMSO, 1951–date
Law Society of Upper Canada, ONTARIO LEGAL AID PLAN: ANNUAL
    REPORT Toronto: 1968–date
Legal Action Group REPRESENTATION BEFORE TRIBUNALS: MEMO–

RANDUM   LAG, 1974

Matthews, E.J.T., and Outlon, A.D.M.   LEGAL AID AND ADVICE UNDER
    THE LEGAL AID AND ADVICE ACTS, 1949-1964   Butterworth,
    1971 (Supplement, 1975)

Moeran, E.   PRACTICAL LEGAL AID (2nd ed)   Oyez, 1976

Ontario Joint Committee on Legal Aid   REPORT   Toronto: Queen's Printer,
    1965

Ontario Task Force on Legal Aid   REPORT   (Chairman: John H. Osler)
    Toronto: Queen's Printer, 1974

Paterson, A.   LEGAL AID AS A SOCIAL SERVICE   Cobden Trust, 1970

Pollock, S.   LEGAL AID: THE FIRST 25 YEARS   Oyez Publishing, 1975

Sachs, E.   LEGAL AID: AN INTRODUCTION TO THE WORKING AND
    PROVISIONS OF THE LEGAL AID AND ADVICE ACT, 1949
    Eyre & Spottiswoode, 1951

Sackville, R.   LEGAL AID IN AUSTRALIA   Canberra: Australian Govt.
    Pub. Service, 1975

Schachter, R.D.   LEGAL AID HANDBOOK   Toronto: Carswell, 1975

Scotland, Committee on Legal Aid in Criminal Proceedings   REPORT   (Cmnd.
    1015) Edinburgh: HMSO, 1960

Wilkins, J.L.   LEGAL AID IN THE CRIMINAL COURTS   Toronto: Univer-
    sity of Toronto Press, 1975

(c)   LEGAL COSTS

Brenchley, A.T.G.   MAGISTERIAL COSTS AND APPLICATION OF PEN—
    ALTIES (3rd ed) Shaw & Sons, 1966

British Columbia Law Reform Commission   REPORT ON CIVIL
    PROCEDURE: PART 1: COSTS OF SUCCESSFUL UNASSISTED
    LAY LITIGANTS   Vancouver: The Commission, 1975

Canada Law Reform Commission   CRIMINAL PROCEDURE: A PROPOSAL
    FOR COSTS IN CRIMINAL CASES   Ottawa: Law Reform Comm-
    ission, 1973

Graham-Green, G.J.   CRIMINAL COSTS INCULDING LEGAL AID   Butter-
    worths, 1965

G.B. Council on Tribunals   REPORT ON THE AWARD OF COSTS AT
    STATUTORY INQUIRIES   HMSO, 1964

Rainbrid, H.J.C. (ed)   BUTTERWORTH'S COSTS IN CIVIL LITIGATION
    (3rd ed) (& Supplements) Butterworths, 1966

Robinson, J.L.R.   COUNTY COURT COSTS (4th ed)   Oyez Publications
    Ltd., 1971

(d) LAW AND SOCIAL WORK

Archer, P. (ed) SOCIAL WELFARE AND THE CITIZEN Harmondsworth: Penguin, 1957

Bailey, R. & Brake, M. (eds) RADICAL SOCIAL WORK, Edward Arnold, 1975

Birrell, W.D. et al. (eds) SOCIAL ADMINISTRATION: READINGS IN APPLIED SOCIAL SCIENCE Harmondsworth: Penguin, 1973

Bradway, J.S. LAW AND SOCIAL WORK Chicago, Ill: University of Chicago Press, 1929

Breckinridge, S.P. SOCIAL WORK AND THE COURTS Chicago, Ill: University of Chicago Press, 1934

Carins, H. LAW AND THE SOCIAL SCIENCES New York: A.M. Kelley, 1969

Family Welfare Association, GUIDE TO THE SOCIAL SERVICES: A BOOK OF INFORMATION REGARDING THE STATUTORY AND VOL-UNTARY SERVICES Macdonald and Evans, annual

Goodlad, S. (ed) EDUCATION AND SOCIAL ACTION Allen & Unwin, 1975

G.B. Home Dept. Committee on Social Services in Courts of Summary Jurisdiction REPORT (Chairman: S.W. Harris) (Cmd. 5122) HMSO, 1936

Guild, M.B. LAWYERS' HELP WITH SOCIAL ASPECTS OF SOCIO–LEGAL PROBLEMS (M.S.W. Thesis) University of Toronto, 1962

Harris, B. LEGAL AID AND ADVICE: A GUIDE FOR MAGISTRATES AND SOCIAL WORKERS Chichester: Barry Rose, 1975

Heywood, J.S., and Allen, B.K. FINANCIAL HELP IN SOCIAL WORK Manchester: Manchester University Press, 1971

Hoggett, B. MENTAL HEALTH Sweet & Maxwell, 1976

Le Mesurier, L. (ed) A HANDBOOK OF PROBATION AND SOCIAL WORK OF THE COURTS National Association of Probation Officers, 1935 (Supplement, 1944)

Levy, R.J. CASES AND MATERIALS ON SOCIAL WELFARE AND THE INDIVIDUAL Mineola, N.Y: Foundation Press, 1971

Marsh, D.C. AN INTRODUCTION TO THE STUDY OF SOCIAL ADMINI-STRATION Routledge & Kegan Paul, 1965

Mathieson, D. and Walker, A. SOCIAL ENQUIRY REPORTS National Association of Probation Officers, 1972

Mayer, J.E. & Timms, N. THE CLIENT SPEAKS Routledge & Kegan Paul, 1970

Perry, F.G. A GUIDE TO THE PREPARATION OF SOCIAL INQUIRY RE-PORTS Chichester: Barry Rose, 1975

Riesenfeld, S.A. MODERN SOCIAL LEGISLATION Brooklyn: Foundation Press, 1950 (Replacement Pamphlet, 1958)

Rios, B.J. (compiler) PLANNING FOR JUSTICE IN SOCIAL WELFARE (Bibliography) Monticello, Ill: Council of Planning Librarians, 1971

Samuels, A. LAW FOR SOCIAL WORKERS Butterworths, 1963

Slack, K.M. SOCIAL ADMINISTRATION AND THE CITIZEN, Michael Joseph, 1966

Smith, C. & Hoath, D.C. LAW AND THE UNDERPRIVILEGED Routledge & Kegan Paul, 1975

Terry, J. A GUIDE TO THE CHILDREN ACT Sweet & Maxwell, 1976

Venables, H.D.S. A GUIDE TO THE LAW AFFECTING MENTAL PATIENTS Butterworths, 1975

Warham, J. AN INTRODUCTION TO ADMINISTRATION FOR SOCIAL WORKERS Routledge & Kegan Paul, 1967

Willmott, P. CONSUMERS' GUIDE TO THE BRITISH SOCIAL SERVICES (2nd ed) Harmondsworth: Penguin, 1971

Zander, M. SOCIAL WORKERS, THEIR CLIENTS AND THE LAW (2nd ed. 1977) Sweet & Maxwell, 1974

(e)   LEGAL PROFESSION

Association of American Law Schools: Curriculum Study Project Committee TRAINING FOR THE PUBLIC PROFESSIONS OF THE LAW: 1971 Washington, 1971

Auerbach, J.S. UNEQUAL JUSTICE: LAWYERS & SOCIAL CHANGE IN MODERN AMERICA New York: Oxford University Press, 1976

Black, J. (ed) RADICAL LAWYERS New York: Avon Publishers, 1971

Boulton, W.W. A GUIDE TO CONDUCT AND ETIQUETTE AT THE BAR OF ENGLAND AND WALES (5th ed) Butterworths, 1971

Campbell,C.M. & Wilson, R.J. PUBLIC ATTITUDES TO THE LEGAL PRO— FESSION IN SCOTLAND for Law Society of Scotland, but as yet unpublished

Carlin, J.E. LAWYERS ON THEIR OWN New Brunswick, N.J.: Rutgers University Press, 1962

Carlin, J.E. LAWYER'S ETHICS New York: Russell Sage Foundation, 1966

Carr-Saunders, A.M. & Wilson, P.A. THE PROFESSIONS Oxford, 1933

Council of the Law Society A GUIDE TO THE PROFESSIONAL CONDUCT OF SOLICITORS Law Society, 1974

Eisenmann, C. THE UNIVERSITY TEACHING OF SOCIAL SCIENCES: LAW (Rev. ed) Paris: UNESCO, 1973

Fitzgerald, J.M. POVERTY AND THE LEGAL PROFESSION IN VICTORIA Canberra: Australian Govt. Print Serv., 1976

Fleming, D. & Bailyn, B. (eds) LAW IN AMERICAN HISTORY Cambridge, Mass: Charles Warren Center for Studies in American History, Harvard, 1971

Ginger, A.F. (ed) THE RELEVANT LAWYERS New York: Simon & Schuster, 1972

G.B. Committee on Legal Education REPORT (Chairman: Mr. Justice Ormrod) (Cmnd. 4595) HMSO, 1971

G.B. National Board for Prices and Incomes REPORT No. 54: REMUNERA—TION OF SOLICITORS (Cmnd. 3529) HMSO, 1968

G.B. National Board for Prices and Incomes REPORT No. 134: REMUNER—ATION OF SOLICITORS (Cmnd. 4217) HMSO, 1969

G.B. National Board for Prices and Incomes, REPORT No. 164: REMUNER—ATION OF SOLICITORS (Cmnd. 4624) HMSO, 1969

Handler, J.F. THE LAWYER AND HIS COMMUNITY Madison, Wis: University of Wisconsin Press, 1967

Hurst, J.W. THE GROWTH OF AMERICAN LAW: THE LAWMAKERS Boston: Little, Brown, 1950

James, M. THE PEOPLE'S LAWYERS New York: Holt, Rinehart & Winston, 1973

Johnson, T.J. PROFESSIONS AND POWER Macmillan, 1972

Johnstone, Q. and Hopson, D. LAWYERS AND THEIR WORK: AN ANALYSIS OF THE LEGAL PROFESSION IN THE UNITED STATES AND ENGLAND Indianapolis: Bobbs-Merrill, 1967

JUSTICE COMPLAINTS AGAINST LAWYERS (Chairman: G. Garrett) Charles Knight, 1970

Klein, R. COMPLAINTS AGAINST DOCTORS: A STUDY IN PROFE—SSIONAL ACCOUNTABILITY Charles Knight, 1973

Lees, D.S. ECONOMIC CONSEQUENCES OF THE PROFESSIONS Institute of Economic Affairs, 1966

Lefcourt, R. (ed) LAW AGAINST THE PEOPLE New York: Random House, 1971

Lochner, P.R. LEARNING TO BE A LAWYER: HOMOGENIZATION AND DIFFERENTATION INTO PUBLIC AND PRIVATE SECTOR PRO—FESSIONAL RULES (Stanford University Thesis, 1971) Ann Arbor, Mich: University Microfilms, 1974

Marks, F.R. THE LAWYER, THE PUBLIC AND PROFESSIONAL RES—PONSIBILITY Chicago: American Bar Foundation, 1972

Maru, O. RESEARCH ON THE LEGAL PROFESSION: REVIEW OF WORK DONE Chicago: American Bar Foundation, 1972

Pound, R. ESSAYS ON THE LEGAL PROFESSION Notre Dame, Ind: Notre Dame Law School, 1944

Pritt, D.N. THE SUBSTANCE OF THE LAW Lawrence & Wishart, 1972

Pritt, D.N. AUTOBIOGRAPHY Lawrence & Wishart, 1965-66

Sanctuary, G. BEFORE YOU SEE A SOLICITOR Oyez Publishing Ltd., 1973

Smigel, E.O. THE WALL STREET LAWYER Bloomington: Indiana University Press, 1964

Society of Labour Lawyers LEGAL EDUCATION Fabian Society, 1969

Warkov, S. LAWYERS IN THE MAKING Chicago: Aldine Pub. Co., 1965

Wasserstein, B. and Green, M. (eds) WITH JUSTICE FOR SOME Boston: Beacon Press, 1970

Weyrauch, W. THE PERSONALITY OF LAWYERS New Haven: Yale University Press, 1964

Zander, M. LAWYERS AND THE PUBLIC INTEREST L.S.E., 1968

Zander, M. THE LEGAL PROFESSION AND THE POOR 20 N.I.L.Q. 109, 1969

(f) PRISONERS' LEGAL RIGHTS

American Bar Assoiciation, Commission on Correctional Facilities and Services PRISONERS' LEGAL RIGHTS: A BIBLIOGRAPHY Washington, D.C: Prison Law Reporter, 1974

G.B. Parliamentary Commissioner for Administration ANNUAL REPORT FOR 1970 pp. 124-7 (H.C. 261/1970-71) HMSO, 1971

Kerper, H.B. LEGAL RIGHTS OF THE CONVICTED St. Paul, Minn: West Pub. Co., 1974

Singer, R.G. and Statsky, W.P. RIGHTS OF THE IMPRISONED Indianapolis: Bobbs-Merrill, 1974

Wexler, D.B. CASES AND MATERIALS ON PRISON INMATE LEGAL ASSISTANCE Washington, D.C: National Institute of Law Enforcement and Criminal Justice, 1973

(g) ENGLISH LEGAL SYSTEM

Abel-Smith, B. and Stevens, R. IN SEARCH OF JUSTICE Allen Lane, 1968

Abel-Smith, B. and Stevens, R. LAWYERS AND THE COURTS Heinemann, 1967

'Barrister' JUSTICE IN ENGLAND Gollancz, 1938

Blumberg, A. THE SCALES OF JUSTICE New Brunswick, N.J: Transaction Inc., 1970

Calvert, H.G. THE WELFARE LEGAL SYSTEM Newcastle upon Tyne: University of Newcastle upon Tyne, 1973

Freeman, M.D. THE LEGAL STRUCTURE Longman, 1974

Friedman, L.W. THE LEGAL SYSTEM: A SOCIAL SCIENCE PERSPEC–
TIVE N.Y: Russell Sage Foundation, 1975

Jackson, R.M. THE MACHINERY OF JUSTICE IN ENGLAND (6th ed)
Cambridge University Press, 1972

Justice, GOING TO LAW: A CRITIQUE OF ENGLISH CIVIL PROCEDURE
Stevens, 1973

Lewis, D. and Hughman, P. JUST HOW JUST? Secker & Warburg, 1975

Mullins, C. IN QUEST OF JUSTICE J. Murray, 1931

Radcliffe, G.R.Y. and Cross, G. ENGLISH LEGAL SYSTEM (5th ed)
by Lord Cross and G.J. Hand Butterworths, 1971

Scarman, Sir L.G. ENGLISH LAW – THE NEW DIMENSION Stevens,
1974

Walker, R.J. and Walker, M.G. ENGLISH LEGAL SYSTEM (3rd ed) Butterworths, 1972

Wilson, G. CASES AND MATERIALS ON THE ENGLISH LEGAL SYSTEM
Sweet & Maxwell, 1973

Zander, M. CASES AND MATERIALS ON THE ENGLISH LEGAL SYSTEM
Weidenfeld & Nicolson, 1973 (2nd ed., 1976)

Zander, M. (ed) WHAT'S WRONG WITH THE LAW B.B.C., 1970

(See also: Westergaard et. al., pp. 11-18, 21-24, 43, 74-78, 79-82, 87-92;
and Blackstone, Part I passim; Ch. XIV and Ch. XV)

(a)   MEANS-TESTED BENEFITS – SUPPLEMENTARY BENEFITS,
         FAMILY INCOME SUPPLEMENT, ETC.

Adler, M. and Bradley, A. (eds) JUSTICE, DISCRETION AND POVERTY:
         SUPPLEMENTARY BENEFIT APPEAL TRIBUNALS IN BRITAIN
         Professional Books, 1975
Atkinson, A.B. POVERTY IN BRITAIN AND THE REFORM OF SOCIAL
         SECURITY Cambridge University Press, 1969
Bell, K. RESEARCH STUDY ON SUPPLEMENTARY BENEFIT APPEAL
         TRIBUNALS.   REVIEW OF MAIN FINDINGS: CONCLUSIONS:
         RECOMMENDATIONS HMSO, 1975
Bond, N. KNOWLEDGE OF RIGHTS AND EXTENT OF UNMET NEED
         AMONGST RECIPIENTS OF SUPPLEMENTARY BENEFITS
         Coventry: Community Development Project, 1972
Bottomley, V.   FAMILIES WITH LOW INCOME IN LONDON   C.P.A.G.,
         1971
Brooke, R. RIGHTS IN THE WELFARE STATE C.P.A.G., 1970
Coleman, R.J. SUPPLEMENTARY BENEFITS AND THE ADMINISTRA–
         TIVE REVIEW OF ADMINISTRATIVE ACTION C.P.A.G., 1971
Elks, L. THE WAGE STOP: POOR BY ORDER C.P.A.G., 1974
Field, F. and Grieve, M. ABUSE AND THE ABUSED C.P.A.G., 1972
Fulbrook, J. THE APPELLANT AND HIS CASE C.P.A.G., 1975
Gearing, B. and Sharp, G. EXCEPTIONAL NEEDS PAYMENTS AND
         THE EDERLY Coventry: Community Development Project, 1974
G.B. Committee on Abuse of Social Security Benefits REPORT (Chairman:
         Sir H. Fisher) (Cmnd. 5228) HMSO, 1973
G.B. Department of Health & Social Security CIRCUMSTANCES OF
         FAMILIES HMSO, 1967
G.B. Expenditure Committee THIRD REPORT. EDUCATIONAL MAIN–
         TENANCE ALLOWANCES IN THE 16-18 YEARS AGE GROUP
         (H.C. 306/1974, Replies by Government in H.C. 262/1974-75)
         HMSO, 1975
G.B. Government PROPOSALS FOR A TAX CREDIT SYSTEM (Cmnd.
         5116) HMSO, 1972
G.B. Supplementary Benefits Commission ADMINISTRATION OF THE
         WAGE-STOP HMSO, 1967
G.B. Supplementary Benefits Commission COHABITATION HMSO, 1971
         (2nd ed., 1976)

G.B. Supplementary Benefits Commission TRAINING OF STAFF   HMSO, 1973

G.B. Supplementary Benefits Commission   EXCEPTIONAL NEEDS PAY—MENTS   HMSO, 1973

G.B. Supplementary Benefits Commission HANDBOOK (4th ed) HMSO, 1974

G.B. Supplementary Benefits Commission REPORT OF THE SUPPLEMEN—TARY BENEFITS COMMISSION YEAR ENDED 31 DECEMBER 1974   HMSO, 1975

G.B. Working Party in Educational Maintenance Allowances REPORT (Chairman: T. Weaver) HMSO, 1957

Herman, M. ADMINISTRATIVE JUSTICE AND SUPPLEMENTARY BENE—FITS Occasional Papers on Social Administration No. 47   Bell & Son, 1972

Howe, J.R. TWO PARENT FAMILIES: A STUDY OF THEIR RESOURCES AND NEEDS IN 1968, 1969 and 1970   D.H.S.S., Statistical Report Series No. 14   HMSO, 1971

Howell, R. WHY WORK? A CHALLENGE TO THE CHANCELLOR   Conservative Political Centre, 1976

Jennings, W.I. THE POOR LAW CODE AND LAW OF UNEMPLOYMENT ASSISTANCE   Chas. Knight & Co. Ltd., 1936

Jordan, B. PAUPERS: THE MAKING OF THE NEW CLAIMING CLASS   Routledge & Kegan Paul, 1973

Kincaid, J.C. POVERTY AND EQUALITY IN BRITAIN: A STUDY OF SOCIAL SECURITY AND TAXATION Harmondsworth: Penguin, 1973

Knight, I.B. and Nixon, J.M. TWO PARENT FAMILIES IN RECEIPT OF FAMILY INCOME SUPPLEMENT, 1972. A STUDY ENQUIRING INTO THE FINANCIAL AND MATERIAL CIRCUMSTANCES OF TWO PARENT FAMILIES RECEIVING F.I.S.   HMSO, 1975

Lister, R. SUPPLEMENTARY BENEFIT RIGHTS   Arrow, 1974

Lister, R. TAKE-UP OF MEANS-TESTED BENEFITS   C.P.A.G., 1974

Lister, R. THE ADMINISTRATION OF THE WAGE STOP   C.P.A.G., 1972

Lister, R. AS MAN AND WIFE? A STUDY OF THE COHABITATION RULE   C.P.A.G., 1973   •

Lister, R. JUSTICE FOR THE CLAIMANT: A STUDY OF SUPPLEMEN—TARY BENEFIT APPEAL TRIBUNALS   C.P.A.G., 1974

Lynes, T. NATIONAL ASSISTANCE AND NATIONAL PROSPERITY   Welwyn: Codicote Press, 1962

Lynes, T. PENGUIN GUIDE TO SUPPLEMENTARY BENEFITS (2nd ed)   Harmondsworth: Penguin, 1974

Marshall, R. FAMILIES RECEIVING SUPPLEMENTARY BENEFIT, D.H.S.S. Statistical and Report Series No. 1   HMSO, 1972

Meacher, M. RATE REBATES: A STUDY OF THE EFFECTIVENESS OF MEANS TESTS C.P.A.G., 1972

Millett, J.D. THE UNEMPLOYMENT ASSISTANCE BOARD Allen & Unwin, 1940

Page, R. THE BENEFITS RACKET Tom Stacey, 1971

Piven, F. and Cloward, R. REGULATING THE POOR Tavistock, 1972

Stevenson, O. CLAIMANT OR CLIENT? Allen & Unwin, 1973

Stocker, E.O.F. and Nilsson, P.C. LAW RELATING TO SUPPLEMENTARY BENEFITS AND FAMILY INCOME SUPPLEMENTS HMSO, 1972 (loose-leaf, up-dated)

(b) OTHER SOCIAL SECURITY BENEFITS: NATIONAL INSURANCE

Aikin, O. and Reid, J. EMPLOYMENT, WELFARE AND SAFETY AT WORK Harmondsworth: Penguin, 1971

Atiyah, P.S. ACCIDENTS, COMPENSATION AND THE LAW (2nd ed) Weidenfield & Nicolson, 1976

Armstrong, S., Mossman, M.J. and Sackville, R. ESSAYS ON LAW AND POVERTY: BAIL AND SOCIAL SECURITY Canberra: Australian Govt. Print Serv., 1976

Australian National Rehabilitation and Compensation Scheme Committee of Inquiry COMPENSATION AND REHABILITATION IN AUS– TRALIA: REPORT Canberra: Australian Govt. Pub. Service, 1974

Baum, D.J. THE FINAL PLATEAU: THE BETRAYAL OF OUR OLDER CITIZENS Toronto: Burns & MacEachern, 1974

Bell, J.S. HOW TO GET YOUR INDUSTRIAL INJURIES BENEFIT Sweet & Maxwell, 1966

Beveridge, Sir W. SOCIAL INSURANCE AND ALLIED SERVICES (Cmd. 6404) HMSO, 1942

Boulton, A.H. THE LAW AND PRACTICE OF SOCIAL SECURITY Bristol: Jordan, 1972

Brockman, J. St. L. LAW RELATING TO FAMILY ALLOWANCES AND NATIONAL INSURANCE (revised and edited by P.C. Nilsson) HMSO, 1973 (loose-leaf, up-dated)

Calvert, H. SOCIAL SECURITY LAW Sweet & Maxwell, 1974

College of Law WELFARE LAW AND PRACTICE College of Law, 1975

Deutsch, A. INCOME REDISTRIBUTION THROUGH CANADIAN FED– ERAL FAMILY ALLOWANCES AND OLD AGE BENEFITS Toronto: Canadian Tax Foundation, 1968

Dixon, R.G. SOCIAL SECURITY, DISABILITY AND MASS JUSTICE New York: Praeger, 1973

Douglas-Mann, B.   ACCIDENTS AT WORK, COMPENSATION FOR ALL
Society of Labour Lawyers, 1974

Emmerson, H.C. and Lascelles, E.C.P.   GUIDE TO THE UNEMPLOYMENT
INSURANCE ACTS (4th ed)   Longmans, Green, 1935

G.B. Committee on the Taxation Treatment of Provisions for Retirement
REPORT   (Cmd. 9063)   HMSO, 1954

G.B. Department of Health & Social Security   BETTER PENSIONS   (Cmnd.
5713)   HMSO, 1974

G.B. National Joint Advisory Council   PRESERVATION OF PENSION ON
CHANGES OF EMPLOYMENT   HMSO, 1966

G.B. Royal Commission on Unemployment Insurance   FIRST AND FINAL
REPORTS (Chairman: H. Gregory) (Cmd. 3872, 4185)   HMSO,
1931

Gibson, M.B.   UNEMPLOYMENT INSURANCE IN GREAT BRITAIN   Allen
& Unwin, 1931

Grunfeld, C.   THE LAW OF REDUNDANCY   Sweet & Maxwell, 1971

Hanes, D.G.   THE FIRST BRITISH WORKMAN'S COMPENSATION ACT,
1897   New Haven: Yale U.P., 1968

Hepple, B. and O'Higgins, P.   INDIVIDUAL EMPLOYMENT LAW   Sweet
& Maxwell, 1971

Hepple, B. and O'Higgins, P.   ENCYCLOPAEDIA OF LABOUR RELATIONS
LAW   Sweet & Maxwell, 1972 (with loose-leaf updating)

Hickling, M.A.   LABOUR DISPUTES AND UNEMPLOYMENT INSURANCE
BENEFITS IN CANADA AND ENGLAND   Don Mills, Ontario:
C.C.H., Canadian, c 1975

Hill, M.   POLICIES FOR THE UNEMPLOYED: HELP OR COERCION?
C.P.A.G., 1974

Illinois University Law Library   SUBJECT BIBLIOGRAPHY ON SOCIAL
SECURITY AND PROGRAMS RELATED TO CHILD WELFARE,
HEALTH INSURANCE AND INCOME MAINTENANCE   Progressive
Center for Comparative Legal Research, Urbana, 1974

Ison, T.G.   THE FORENSIC LOTTERY   Staples, 1967

Jenkins, E. (ed)   DIGEST OF (NATIONAL INSURANCE) COMMISSIONERS'
DECISIONS   HMSO, 1964

JUSTICE   NO FAULT ON THE ROADS (Chairman: P. Sieghart)   Stevens,
1974

Kahn-Freund, O. and Hepple, B.   LAWS AGAINST STRIKES   Fabian
Society, 1972

Lister, R. (ed)   NATIONAL WELFARE BENEFITS HANDBOOK (6th ed)
C.P.A.G., 1976

Moore, P.   UNEMPLOYED WORKERS AND STRIKERS: GUIDE TO
SOCIAL SECURITY (CPAG Rights Guide No. 1)   C.P.A.G., 1975

Moore, P.   STUDENTS' RIGHTS (CPAG Rights Guide No. 2)   C.P.A.G.,

1975

Parker, S.R. et. al. EFFECTS OF THE REDUNDANCY PAYMENTS ACT
HMSO, 1971

Potter, D. (ed) THE NATIONAL INSURANCE ACT, 1946 Butterworth,
1946

Potter, D. and Stansfield, D.H. NATIONAL INSURANCE (2nd ed) Butterworth, 1949

Rideout, W.R. REFORMING THE REDUNDANCY PAYMENTS ACT Institute of Personnel Management, 1969

Riesenfeld, S.A. and Maxwell, R.C. MODERN SOCIAL LEGISLATION
Brooklyn: Foundation Press, 1950

Robson, W.A. (ed) SOCIAL SECURITY (3rd ed) Allen & Unwin, 1948

Ruegg, A.H. (ed) EMPLOYER'S LIABILITY ACT 1880 AND WORKMEN'S
COMPENSATION ACTS, 1897 & 1900 (6th ed) Butterworth, 1903

Samuels, H. REDUNDANCY PAYMENTS: AN ANNOTATION AND GUIDE
TO THE REDUNDANCY PAYMENTS ACT, 1965 Charles Knight,
1970

Samuels, H. and Stewart-Pearson, N. REDUNDANCY PAYMENTS (2nd ed)
Charles Knight, 1970

Shannon, N.P. THE NATIONAL INSURANCE (INDUSTRIAL INJURIES)
ACT, 1946 (With general introduction and annotations by N.P.
Shannon and D. Potter) Butterworth, 1946

Smith, N.J. A BRIEF GUIDE TO SOCIAL LEGISLATION Methuen, 1972

Society of Labour Lawyers OCCUPATIONAL ACCIDENTS AND THE LAW
Fabian Society, 1970

Thieblet, A.J. and Cowin, R.M. WELFARE AND STRIKES Philadelphia
Industrial Research Unit, Wharton School of Finance and Commerce,
University of Pennsylvania, 1972

Vadakin, J.C. CHILDREN, POVERTY AND FAMILY ALLOWANCES New
York: Basic Books, 1968

Vester, H. and Cartwright, H.A. INDUSTRIAL INJURIES (2 vols) Sweet
& Maxwell, 1961

Walley, Sir J. SOCIAL SECURITY: ANOTHER BRITISH FAILURE? Charles
Knight, 1972

Webb, E.A. INDUSTRIAL INJURIES: A NEW APPROACH Fabian Society,
1974

Whincup, M.H. REDUNDANCY AND THE LAW Pergamon Press, Oxford,
1967

Willis, W.A. (ed) THE WORKMEN'S COMPENSATION ACT, 1906 Butter-
woth, 1919

Young, A.F. INDUSTRIAL INJURIES INSURANCE Routledge & Kegan
Paul, 1964

(c)   SOCIAL WELFARE POLICY: GENERAL

(and see Blackstone, passim)

Abel-Smith, B. SOCIALISM AND AFFLUENCE   Fabian Society, 1967
Abel-Smith, B. & Townsend, P. THE POOR AND THE POOREST Bell,
      1965
Adams, I. THE POVERTY WALL   Toronto: McClelland & Stewart, 1970
Atkinson, A.B. THE ECONOMICS OF INEQUALITY   Oxford University
      Press, 1974
Atkinson, A.B. POVERTY IN BRITAIN AND THE REFORM OF SOCIAL
      SECURITY Cambridge University Press, 1969
Batchelder, A.B. THE ECONOMICS OF POVERTY   New York: Wiley,
      1966
Boyson, R. (ed) DOWN WITH THE POOR   Churchill Press, 1971
Brown, R.G.S. THE MANAGEMENT OF WELFARE   Fontana, 1975
Bruce, M. THE COMING OF THE WELFARE STATE (4th ed)   Batsford,
      1968
Bruce, M. (ed) THE RISE OF THE WELFARE STATE: ENGLISH SOCIAL
      POLICY 1601-1971 Weidenfeld & Nicolson, 1973
Bull, D. (ed) FAMILY POVERTY (2nd ed) Duckworth, 1972
Butterworth, E. & Holman, R. (eds) SOCIAL WELFARE IN MODERN
      BRITAIN Fontana, 1975
Canada, Special Senate Committee on Poverty POVERTY IN CANADA:
      REPORT Ottawa: Information Canada, 1971
Coates, K. & Silburn, R. POVERTY: THE FORGOTTEN ENGLISHMAN
      Harmondsworth: Penguin, 1973
Checkland, S.E. & E.O.A. (eds) THE POOR LAW OF 1834
      Harmondsworth: Penguin, 1974
Christopher, A. et al. POLICY FOR POVERTY: A STUDY OF THE
      URGENCY OF REFORM IN SOCIAL BENEFITS AND OF THE
      ADVANTAGES AND LIMITATIONS OF A REVERSE INCOME
      TAX IN REPLACEMENT OF THE EXISTING STRUCTURE OF
      STATE BENEFITS Institute of Economic Affairs, 1970
Coll, B.D. PERSPECTIVES IN PUBLIC WELFARE: A HISTORY   Washing-
      ton: U.S. Govt. Print Off., 1969
Davies, B. SOCIAL NEEDS AND RESOURCES IN LOCAL SERVICES
      Joseph, 1968
Field, F. (ed) LOW PAY Arrow, 1973
Field, F. UNEQUAL BRITAIN: A REPORT ON THE CYCLE OF IN—
      EQUALITY Arrow, 1974
Fisher, A. & Dix, B. LOW PAY AND HOW TO END IT: A UNION VIEW
      Pitman, 1974

Fraser, D. THE EVOLUTION OF THE BRITISH WELFARE STATE: A HISTORY OF SOCIAL POLICY SINCE THE INDUSTRIAL REVO-LUTION Macmillan, 1973

George, V. SOCIAL SECURITY: BEVERIDGE AND AFTER Routledge & Kegan Paul, 1968

George, V. SOCIAL SECURITY AND SOCIETY Routledge & Kegan Paul, 1973

G.B. Department of Employment & Productivity A NATIONAL MINIMUM WAGE: AN INQUIRY HMSO, 1969

G.B. Expenditure Committee EXPENDITURE CUTS IN HEALTH AND PERSONAL SOCIAL SERVICES (H.C. 307/1974) HMSO, 1975

G.B. National Board for Prices and Incomes GENERAL PROBLEMS OF LOW PAY (Report No. 169, Cmnd. 4648) HMSO, 1971

G.B. Royal Commission on Equal Pay REPORT (Chairman: C. Asquith) (Cmd. 6937) HMSO, 1946

Gould, T. & Kenyon, J. STORIES FROM THE DOLE QUEUE Temple Smith, 1972

Hall, P., Land, H., Parker, R. & Webb, A. CHANGE, CHOICE AND CONFLICT IN SOCIAL POLICY Heinemann, 1975

Harrington, M. THE OTHER AMERICA: POVERTY IN THE UNITED STATES New York: Macmillan, 1962

Kershaw, J.A. GOVERNMENT AGAINST POVERTY Washington D.C: The Brookings Institution, 1970

La France, A.B. and others LAW OF THE POOR St. Paul, Minn: West Pub. Co., 1973

Marris, P. and Rein, M. DILEMMAS OF SOCIAL REFORM (2nd ed) Harmondsworth: Penguin, 1972

Marsh, D.C. THE FUTURE OF THE WELFARE STATE Harmondsworth: Penguin, 1964

Mencher, S. POOR LAW TO POVERTY PROGRAM: ECONOMIC SECURITY POLICY IN BRITAIN AND THE U.S. Pittsburgh: University of Pittsburgh Press, 1967

Meriam, L. RELIEF AND SOCIAL SECURITY Washington D.C: The Brookings Institution, 1946

National Conference on Law & Poverty, 1965 CONFERENCE PRO-CEEDINGS Washington, D.C: U.S. Govt. Print Off., 1966

Organization for Economic Cooperation and Development NEGATIVE IN-COME TAX Paris: O.E.C.D., 1974

Polonyi, G. and Wood, J.B. HOW MUCH INEQUALITY? Institute of Economic Affairs, 1974

Poynter, J.R. SOCIETY AND PAUPERISM: ENGLISH IDEAS ON POOR RELIEF, 1795-1834 Routledge & Kegan Paul, 1969

Prest, A.R. SOCIAL BENEFITS AND TAX RATES: A SHORT STUDY OF

IMPLICIT AND EXPLICIT MARGINAL TAX RATES IN ENGLAND
AND WALES   Institute of Economic Affairs, 1970

Roach, J.L. and Roach, J.K. (eds) POVERTY: SELECTED READINGS
Harmondsworth: Penguin, 1972

Roberts, D. VICTORIAN ORIGINS OF THE BRITISH WELFARE STATE
Hamden, Conn: Archon Books, 1969

Robson, W. and Crick, B. (eds) THE FUTURE OF THE SOCIAL SERVICES
Harmondsworth: Penguin, 1970

Rodgers, B. THE BATTLE AGAINST POVERTY vols. I and II   Routledge
& Kegan Paul, 1969

Sleeman, J.F. THE WELFARE STATE: ITS AIMS, BENEFITS AND COSTS
Allen & Unwin, 1973

Steiner, G.Y. SOCIAL INSECURITY: THE POLITICS OF WELFARE
Chicago: Rand McNally, 1966

Titmuss, R.M. SOCIAL POLICY: AN INTRODUCTION   Allen & Unwin,
1974

Titmuss, R.   ESSAYS ON 'THE WELFARE STATE' (2nd ed)   Allen &
Unwin, 1963

Titmuss, R.M. INCOME DISTRIBUTION AND SOCIAL CHANGE: A
STUDY IN CRITICISM   Allen & Unwin, 1962

Townsend, P. (ed) THE CONCEPT OF POVERTY   Heinemann, 1970

Townsend, P. et al.   SOCIAL SERVICES FOR ALL?   Fabian Society,
1968

Tullock, G. PRIVATE WANTS, PUBLIC MEANS   New York: Basic Books,
1970

U.S. Social Security Administration, Office of Research and Statistics
POVERTY STUDIES IN THE SIXTIES: A SELECTED, ANNO-
TATED BIBLIOGRAPHY   Washington: U.S. Govt. Print Off.,
1970

Webb, A.L. and Sieve, J.E.B. INCOME REDISTRIBUTIONAND THE
WELFARE STATE   Bell, 1971

Wedderburn, D. (ed) POVERTY, INEQUALITY AND CLASS STRUCTURE
Cambridge University Press, 1974

Young, M. POVERTY REPORTS, 1974, 1975, 1976   Temple Smith,
1974, 1975, 1976

III SELECTED FAMILY LAW ISSUES

(See also Westergaard: pp. 84-87; Blackstone: Ch. IX)

Anthony, E. and Berryman, J.D. LEGAL GUIDE TO DOMESTIC PRO—
CEEDINGS Butterworths, 1968
Barnsley, D.G. HIS, HERS, OR THEIRS? Leicester: University Press,
1975
Bevan, H.K. THE LAW RELATING TO CHILDREN Butterworths, 1973
Bromley, P. FAMILY LAW (4th ed) Butterworth, 1971
Canadian Council on Social Development THE ONE-PARENT FAMILY
Ottawa, 1974
Conservative Political Centre UNHAPPY FAMILIES (Evidence to the Finer
Committee on One-Parent Families) Conservative Political Centre,
1971
Coote, A. and Gill, T. WOMEN'S RIGHTS: A PRACTICAL GUIDE Har-
mondsworth: Penguin, 1974
Council for Children's Welfare A FAMILY SERVICE AND A FAMILY
COURT Council for Children's Welfare, 1966
Eekelaar, J. FAMILY SECURITY AND FAMILY BREAKDOWN Harmonds-
worth: Penguin, 1971
Ferri, E. GROWING UP IN A ONE-PARENT FAMILY National Founda-
tion for Educational Research in England & Wales, 1976
Ferri, E. and Robinson, H. COPING ALONE National Foundation for
Educational Research in England & Wales, 1976
George, V. and Wilding, P. MOTHERLESS FAMILIES Routledge & Kegan
Paul, 1972
Gill, T. and Coote, A. BATTERED WOMEN: HOW TO USE THE LAW
National Council for Civil Liberties, 1975
G.B. Committee on One-Parent Families REPORT (Chairman: Sir M. Finer)
(Cmnd. 5629) HMSO, 1974
G.B. Committee on Statutory Maintenance Limits REPORT (Chairman:
Miss J. Graham-Hall) (Cmnd. 3587) HMSO, 1968
G.B. Law Commission FAMILY LAW: FAMILY PROPERTY LAW
(Working Paper No. 42) Law Commission, 1971
G.B. Law Commission FAMILY LAW: 1st REPORT ON FAMILY
PROPERTY (H.C. 274, 1972-73) HMSO, 1973
G.B. Law Commission FAMILY LAW: MATRIMONIAL PROCEEDINGS
IN MAGISTRATES' COURTS (Working Paper No. 53) HMSO,
1973
G.B. Parliament Select Committee on Violence in Marriage REPORT (H.C.
553-1/1974-75, EVIDENCE, H.C. 553(ii)/1974-75) HMSO, 1975
Handler, J.F. (ed) FAMILY LAW AND THE POOR: ESSAYS BY JACOBUS

tenBROEK   Westport, Conn: Greenwood Publishing Corp., 1971

Holman, R. et al. SOCIALLY DEPRIVED FAMILIES IN BRITAIN National
Council For Social Service, 1970

Hunt, A., Fox, J. and Morgan, M. FAMILIES AND THEIR NEEDS HMSO,
1973

Jordan, B. POOR PARENTS: SOCIAL POLICY AND THE 'CYCLE OF
DEPRIVATON'   Routledge & Kegan Paul, 1974

Kemp, M., Knightly, B. and Norton, M. BATTERED WOMEN AND THE
LAW   Interaction Advisory Service, 1975

McGregor, O.R., Blom-Cooper, L, Gibson, C. SEPARATED SPOUSES
Duckworth, 1970

Marsden, D. MOTHERS ALONE   Harmondsworth: Penguin, 1973

Miller, J.G. FAMILY PROPERTY AND FINANCIAL PROVISION Sweet
& Maxwell, 1974

Miller, N. BATTERED SPOUSES (Occasional Paper on Social Administration
No. 57)   Bell, 1975

Paddington Law Centre INJUNCTIONS FOR BATTERED WIVES   Paddington Neighbourhood Law Centre, 1975

Pizzey, E. SCREAM QUIETLY OR THE NEIGHBOURS WILL HEAR
Harmondsworth: Penguin, 1974

Pugh, L.M. MATRIMONIAL PROCEEDINGS BEFORE MAGISTRATES
(2nd ed) Butterworths, 1966

Schlesinger, B. THE ONE-PARENT FAMILY PERSPECTIVES & ANNO—
TATED BIBLIOGRAPHY (2nd ed) Toronto: Toronto University
Press, 1970

Streather, J. and Weir, S. SOCAIL INSECURITY: SINGLE MOTHERS
ON BENEFIT CPAG, 1974

Todd, J.E. and Jones, L.M. MATRIMONIAL PROPERTY   HMSO, 1972

Turner, J.N. IMPROVING THE LOT OF CHILDREN BORN OUTSIDE
MARRIAGE   National Council for One-Parent Families, 1973

Tracey, R. BATTERED WIVES   Conservative Political Centre, 1974

Unger, J. (ed) PARENTAL CUSTODY AND MATRIMONIAL MAINTEN—
ANCE   British Institute of International and Comparative Law, 1966

Wynn, M. FAMILY POLICY: A STUDY OF THE ECONOMIC COSTS OF
REARING CHILDREN AND THEIR SOCIAL AND POLITICAL
CONSEQUENCES   Harmondsworth: Penguin, 1972

Wynn, M. FATHERLESS FAMILIES   Michael Joseph, 1964

IV HOUSING, PROPERTY AND PLANNING

(See also: Westergaard, pp. 21-2; 72-3; 100-109; and Blackstone, pp. 36-37; Ch. XI; pp. 101-102)

(a) HOUSING AND PROPERTY: GENERAL LAW AND POLICY

Ackerman, B.A. ECONOMIC FOUNDATIONS OF PROPERTY LAW
    Boston: Little, Brown, 1975
Alderson, S. BRITAIN IN THE SIXTIES: HOUSING Harmondsworth:
    Penguin, 1962
American Bar Association: Special Committee on Housing and Urban Develop-
    ment Law HOUSING AND URBAN DEVELOPMENT Chicago:
    American Bar Association, 1972
Bailey, R. THE SQUATTERS Harmondsworth: Penguin, 1973
Bailey, R. BED AND BREAKFAST Shelter, 1974
Bailey, R. and Ruddock, J. THE GRIEF REPORT Shelter, 1972
Berry, F. HOUSING: THE GREAT BRITISH FAILURE Knight, 1974
Burney, E. HOUSING ON TRIAL Oxford University Press, 1967
CHAR, ASS, PHAS, SHELTER, EMPTY PROPERTY: A GUIDE FOR
    LOCAL GROUPS Campaign for the Homeless & Rootless, 1975
Canadian Conference on Housing THE RIGHT TO HOUSING (Michael
    Wheeler ed) Montreal: Harvest House, 1969
Chapman, S.D. (ed) THE HISTORY OF WORKING CLASS HOUSING
    Newton Abbot: David & Charles, 1971
Clarke, J.J. THE HOUSING PROBLEM – ITS GROWTH, LEGISLATION
    AND PROCEDURE Pitman, 1920
Commons, J.R. LEGAL FOUNDATIONS OF CAPITALISM New York:
    Macmillan, 1924
Cramond, R.D. HOUSING POLICY IN SCOTLAND 1919-1964 Edin-
    burgh: Oliver and Boyd, 1966
Crosland, A. TOWARDS A LABOUR HOUSING POLICY Fabian Society,
    1971
Cullingworth, J.B. and Karn, V.A. THE OWNERSHIP & MANAGEMENT
    OF HOUSING IN THE NEW TOWNS HMSO, 1968
Cullingworth, J.B. HOUSING IN TRANSITION Heinemann, 1963
Cullingworth, J.B. HOUSING IN GREATER LONDON L.S.E. Greater
    London Papers No. 4, 1961
Cullingworth, J.B. RESTRAINING URBAN GROWTH Fabian Society,
    1961
Cullingworth, J.B. PROBLEMS OF AN URBAN SOCIETY Allen & Unwin,
    1973
Cullingworth, J.B. ENGLISH HOUSING TRENDS (Occasional Papers on

Social Administration No. 13) Bell, 1965

Cullingworth, J.B. HOUSING NEEDS AND PLANNING POLICY Routledge
   1960

Cullingworth, J.B. A PROFILE OF GLASGOW HOUSING, 1965 Edinburgh: Oliver & Boyd, 1968

Denman, D.R. LAND IN THE MARKET (Hobart Paper 30) Institute of
   Economic Affairs, 1964

Denman, D.R. and others CONTEMPORARY PROBLEMS OF LAND
   OWNERSHIP University of Cambridge: Department of Land
   Economy, 1963

Dennis, M. and Fish, S. PROGRAMS IN SEARCH OF A POLICY: LOW
   INCOME HOUSING IN CANADA Toronto: Hakkert, 1972

Dietze, G. IN DEFENSE OF PROPERTY Chicago: H. Regnery Co., 1963

Donnison, D.B. HOUSING POLICY SINCE THE WAR (Occasional Papers
   on Social Administration) Welwyn: Codicote Press, 1960

Donnison, D.V., Cockburn, C. Cullingworth, J.B. and Nevitt, D.A. ESSAYS
   ON HOUSING (Occasional Papers on Social Administration, No. 9)
   Welwyn: Codicote Press, 1964

Donnison, D.V. THE GOVERNMENT OF HOUSING Harmondsworth:
   Penguin, 1967

Furubotu, E.G. (ed) THE ECONOMICS OF PROPERTY RIGHTS
   Cambridge, Mass: Ballinger, 1974

Gauldie, E. CRUEL HABITATIONS Allen & Unwin, 1974

G.B. Department of the Environment FAIR DEAL FOR HOUSING (Cmnd.
   4728) HMSO, 1971

G.B. Department of the Environment WIDENING THE CHOICE: THE NEXT
   STEPS IN HOUSING (Cmnd. 5280) HMSO, 1973

G.B. Department of the Environment BETTER HOMES – THE NEXT PRI–
   ORITIES (Cmnd. 5339) HMSO, 1973

G.B. Law Commission ENTERING AND REMAINING ON PROPERTY
   (Working Paper No. 54) HMSO, 1974

G.B. Ministry of Housing & Local Government THE HOUSING PRO–
   GRAMME 1965-1970 (Cmnd. 2838) HMSO, 1965

G.B. Scottish Development Department HOUSING AND SOCIAL WORK:
   A JOINT APPROACH (Report of Morris Committee) HMSO, 1975

G.B. Select Committee on Race Relations & Immigration HOUSING (H.C.
   508/1970-71) HMSO, 1971

G.B. Department of the Environment RACE RELATIONS & HOUSING
   (Cmnd. 6232) HMSO, 1975

Greve, J. with others REPORT TO L.C.C. OF INQUIRY INTO HOME–
   LESSNESS L.C.C. Minutes, 7 July 1962

Greve et al. HOMELESSNESS IN LONDON Scottish Academic Press, 1971

Greve, J. LONDON'S HOMELESS (Occasional Papers on Social Administration) Bell, 1964

Glastonbury, B. HOMELESS NEAR A THOUSAND HOMES Allen & Unwin, 1971

Haar, C.M. & Iatridis, D.S. HOUSING THE POOR IN SUBURBIA: PUBLIC POLICY AT THE GRASS ROOTS Cambridge, Mass: Ballinger Pub. Co., 1974

Harloe, M., Issacharoff, R. & Minors, R. THE ORGANIZATION OF HOUSING: PUBLIC AND PRIVATE ENTERPRISE IN LONDON Heinemann, 1974

Hill, O. HOMES OF THE LONDON POOR (new ed) Macmillan, 1883

Joseph, Sir K. CHANGING HOUSING Conservative Political Centre, 1967

Lansley, S. & Fiegehen, G. ONE NATION? HOUSING AND CONSER— VATIVE POLICY Fabian Society, 1974

Larkin, P. PROPERTY IN THE 18th CENTURY New York: H. Fertig, 1969

Lawson, F.H. INTRODUCTION TO THE LAW OF PROPERTY Oxford University Press, 1958

MacColl, J. PLAN FOR HOUSING Fabian Society, 1954

Macrae, N. HOMES FOR THE POEPLE Economic Research Council, 1967

Manne, H.G. THE ECONOMICS OF LEGAL RELATIONSHIPS: READINGS IN THE THEORY OF PROPERTY RIGHTS St. Paul, Minn: West Pub. Co., 1975

Marriott, O. THE PROPERTY BOOM Pan Books, 1967

Matthews, G. KNOWHERE TO GO Canterbury: The Cyrenians, 1974

Meade, J.E. EFFICIENCY, EQUALITY, AND THE OWNERSHIP OF PROPERTY Allen & Unwin, 1964

Merrett, A.J. and Sykes, A. HOUSING FINANCE AND DEVELOPMENT: AN ANALYSIS AND PROGRAMME FOR REFORM Longmans, 1965

Morgan, E.V. THE STRUCTURE OF PROPERTY OWNERSHIP IN GREAT BRITAIN Oxford: Clarendon Press, 1960

Morris, I. and Mogey, J. SOCIOLOGY OF HOUSING Routledge & Kegan Paul, 1965

Needleman, L. THE ECONOMICS OF HOUSING Staples Press, 1965

Netzer, R. ECONOMIC AND URBAN PROBLEMS New York: Basic Books, 1970

Nevitt, A.A. HOUSING, TAXATION AND SUBSIDIES Nelson, 1966

Nevitt, A.A. (ed) THE ECONOMIC PROBLEMS OF HOUSING Macmillan, 1967

Nevitt, D.A. FAIR DEAL FOR HOUSEHOLDERS Fabian Society, 1971

Pennance, F.G. HOUSING MARKET ANALYSIS AND POLICY Institute of Economic Affairs, 1969

Pennance, F.G. and Gray, H. CHOICE IN HOUSING Research Report,

Institute of Economic Affairs, 1968

Pennance, F.G. HOUSING, TOWN PLANNING AND THE LAND COMM—
ISSION (Hobart Paper 40) Institute of Economic Affairs, 1967

Plager, S.J. NEW APPROACHES IN THE LAW OF PROPERTY Mineola,
N.Y: Foundation Press, 1970

Proudhon, P.J. WHAT IS PROPERTY? New York: H. Fertig, 1966

Rex, J. and Moore, R. FACE, COMMUNITY AND CONFLICT Oxford:
University Press, 1969

Rose, H. HOUSING: FOUNDATIONS OF AN EFFECTIVE SERVICE
Fabian Society, 1970

Rose, H. THE HOUSING PROBLEM Heinemann, 1968

Schlatter, R.B. PRIVATE PROPERTY, THE HISTORY OF AN IDEA Allen
& Unwin, 1951

Schorr, A. SLUMS AND SOCIAL INSECURITY Nelson, 1964

Shelter WHO ARE THE HOMELESS? FACE THE FACTS Shelter, 1969

Simpson, A.W.B. AN INTRODUCTION TO THE HISTORY OF LAND LAW
Oxford: University Press, 1961, 1964

Standing Working Party on London Housing LONDON'S HOUSING NEEDS
UP TO 1974 Ministry of Housing & Local Government, 1970

Stegman, M.A. (compiler) HOUSING & ECONOMICS: THE AMERICAN
DILEMMA Cambridge, Mass: M.I.T. Press, 1971

Stein, L.A. URBAN LEGAL PROBLEMS Sydney: Law Book Co., 1974

Turvey, R. THE ECONOMICS OF REAL PROPERTY Allen & Unwin,
1957

U.S. Commission on Civil Rights HOME OWNERSHIP FOR LOWER INCOME
FAMILIES Washington: U.S. Govt. Print Off., 1971

Walters, A.A. et al. GOVERNMENT AND THE LAND Institute of Economic Affairs, 1974

Wendt, P.F. HOUSING POLICY — THE SEARCH FOR SOLUTIONS
Berkeley: University of California Press, 1962

Wicks, M. RENTED HOUSING AND SOCIAL OWNERSHIP Fabian Society,
1973

Wheaton, W.L.C. and others (compiler) HOUSING, RENEWAL AND DEV—
ELOPMENT: BIBLIOGRAPHY Monticello, Ill: Council of Planning
Librarians, 1968

Willshere, N.A.D. RENT, RATES & HOUSING Estates Gazette, 1944

Woolf, M. THE HOUSING SURVEY IN ENGLAND & WALES, 1964
HMSO, 1967

(b)   LOCAL AUTHORITY HOUSING

Bowley, M.E.A. HOUSING AND THE STATE Allen & Unwin, 1945

Burn, D. RENT STRIKE ST. PANCRAS 1960 Pluto Press, 1972

Cullingworth, J.B. HOUSING AND LOCAL GOVERNMENT Allen & Unwin, 1966

Cullingworth, J.B. REPORT TO THE MINISTER OF HOUSING AND LOCAL GOVERNMENT ON THE PROPOSALS FOR TRANSFER OF G.L.C. HOUSING TO THE LONDON BOROUGHS 2 vols. HMSO, 1970

Cramond, R.D. ALLOCATION OF COUNCIL HOUSES Edinburgh: Oliver & Boyd, 1964

Goudie, J. COUNCILS AND THE HOUSING FINANCE ACT Fabian Society, 1972

Gray, H. THE COST OF COUNCIL HOUSING Institute for Economic Affairs, 1968

G.B. Central Housing Advisory Committee COUNCIL HOUSING PURPOSES, PROCEDURES AND PRIORITIES HMSO, 1969

G.B. Central Housing Advisory Committee COUNCILS AND THEIR HOUSES: MANAGEMENT OF ESTATES HMSO, 1959

G.B. Central Housing Advisory Committee RESIDENTIAL QUALIFICATIONS HMSO, 1953

G.B. Central Housing Advisory Committee TRANSFERS, EXCHANGES AND RENTS HMSO, 1953

G.B. Central Housing Advisory Committee UNSATISFACTORY TENANTS HMSO, 1955

G.B. Estimates Committee FOURTH REPORT – HOUSING SUBSIDIES (H.C. 473/1968-69) HMSO, 1969

G.B. Ministry of Housing & Local Government THE HOUSING ROLE OF THE GREATER LONDON COUNCIL WITHIN LONDON HMSO, 1967

G.B. Ministry of Housing & Local Government HOUSING REVENUE ACCOUNTS: REPORT OF THE WORKING PARTY ON THE H.R.A. HMSO, 1969

G.B. Ministry of Housing & Local Government HOUSING SUBSIDIES MANUAL HMSO, 1967

G.B. National Board for Prices & Incomes INCREASES IN RENTS OF LOCAL AUTHORITY HOUSING (Report No. 62) (Cmnd. 3604) HMSO, 1968

G.B. Scottish Development Department RENTS OF HOUSES OWNED BY LOCAL AUTHORITIES IN SCOTLAND, 1970 (Cmnd. 4607) HMSO, 1971

Lefcoe, G. HOUSING FINANCE LAW Indianapolis: Bobbs-Merrill, 1969

Macey, J.P. and Baker, C.V. HOUSING MANAGEMENT The Estates Gazette, 1973

Magnus, S.W. and Tovell, L. (eds) HOUSING FINANCE Knight, 1960

Mandelker, D. HOUSING SUBSIDIES IN THE U.S. & ENGLAND Indianapolis: Bobbs-Merrill, 1973

Parker, P.A. THE HOUSING FINANCE BILL AND COUNCIL TENANTS
    CPAG, 1972

Parker, R. THE RENTS OF COUNCIL HOUSES Bell, 1967

Rhodes, G. (ed) THE NEW GOVERNMENT OF LONDON: THE FIRST FIVE
    YEARS (Ch. 7 on Housing) Weidenfeld & Nicolson, 1972

Skinner, D. and Langdon, J. THE STORY OF CLAY CROSS Nottingham:
    Spokesman Books, 1974

Shelter COVENTRY COUNCIL HOUSES: THE NEW SLUMS Shelter, 1974

Shelter HOMES FIT FOR HEROES: A SHELTER REPORT ON COUNCIL
    HOUSING Shelter, 1975

Stoots, C.F. (compiler) LOCAL HOUSING AUTHORITIES Monticello,
    Ill: Council of Planning Librarians, 1970

Swift, S. HOUSING ADMINISTRATION (4th ed by S. Swift and F. Shaw)
    Butterworth, 1958

Tucker, A.J. HONOURABLE ESTATES Gollancz, 1966

Ward, C. TENANTS TAKE OVER Architectural Press, 1974

York, A. VOLUNTARY ORGANIZATIONS ON A DIFFICULT HOUSING
    ESTATE (unpublished M.A. thesis) University of Leicester, 1972

(c)   LANDLORD/TENANT RELATIONSHIP (PRIVATE)

Abbey, N.C. A COMPANION TO THE NEW LAW OF LANDLORD AND
    TENANT Eyre & Spottiswoode, 1954

Abbey, N.C. RENT ACTS 1920-1957 Eyre & Spottiswoode, 1957

Adams, B. et al. A STUDY OF RENT TRIBUNAL CASES IN LONDON
    (Working Paper No. 68) Centre for Environmental Studies, 1971

Adkin's LANDLORD AND TENANT (17th ed. by Walton, Sir R. and
    Essayan, M.) Estates Gazette Ltd., 1973

Aldridge, T.M. RENT CONTROL AND LEASEHOLD ENFRANCHISEMENT
    (2nd ed) Oyez Publications, 1967

Allaun, F. HEARBREAK HOUSING Hodder & Staughton, 1968

Allaun, F. NO PLACE LIKE HOME Andre Deutsch, 1972

Anon. HOMES TO RENT Association of Land and Property Owners, 1968

Barnes, D.M.W. THE LEASEHOLD REFORM ACT, 1967 Butterworths,
    1968

Barnett, M.J. POLITICS OF LEGISLATION: THE RENT ACT 1957 Weid-
    enfeld & Nicolson, 1969

Block, G.D.M. RENTS IN PERSPECTIVE Conservative Political Centre,
    1961

Blundell, L.A. and Wellings, V.G. RENT RESTRICTIONS GUIDE (4th ed)
    Sweet & Maxwell, 1956

Blundell, L.A. and Wellings, V.G.   THE COMPLETE GUIDE TO THE RENT ACTS   Sweet & Maxwell, 1958

Bramall, A.   THE RENT ACT, 1965   Sweet & Maxwell, 1965

Bramall, A.   A GUIDE TO THE RENT ACT, 1957   Current Law Publishers, 1957

Bradbrook, A.J.   POVERTY AND THE LANDLORD – TENANT RELA-TIONSHIP   Canberra: Australian Govt. Print Service, 1975

Brill, H.   WHY ORGANIZERS FAIL: THE STORY OF A RENT STRIKE   Berkeley: University of California Press, 1971

British Columbia Interdepartmental Study Team on Housing and Rents   HOUSING AND RENT CONTROL IN BRITISH COLUMBIA: A REPORT (Chairman: K. Jaffary)   Vancouver: Interdepartmental Study Team on Housing and Rents, 1975

Burghardt, S.   TENANTS AND THE URBAN HOUSING CRISIS   Dexter, Mich: The New Press, 1972

Canadian Council on Social Development   IS THERE A CASE FOR RENT CONTROL?   Ottawa, 1973

Caplan, D.   PEOPLE AND HOMES: AN INDEPENDENT STUDY OF LAND-LORD AND TENANT RELATIONS, 1974-75   British Property Federation, 1975

Carmichael, J.   VACANT POSSESSION   (Hobart Paper 28)   Institute for Economic Affairs, 1964

Chapman, S.D. (ed)   THE HISTORY OF WORKING CLASS HOUSING   Newton Abbot: David & Charles, 1971

Clark, D. and others   RULES OF THE GAME: A HANDBOOK FOR TENANTS AND HOMEOWNERS   Toronto: Hogtown Press, 1973

Comyn, Sir R.B.   A TREATISE ON THE LAW OF LANDLORD AND TENANT   Saunders & Benning, 1830

Conservative Political Centre   ECLIPSE OF THE PRIVATE LANDLORD: A STUDY OF THE CONSEQUENCES   C.P.C., 1974

Cutting, M.   HOUSING RIGHTS HANDBOOK   Shelter, 1974

Donnison, D.V., Cockburn, C. and Corbett, T.   HOUSING SINCE THE RENT ACT,   (Occasional Paper on Social Administration No. 3) Codicote Press, 1961

Douglas-Mann, B. (Chairman)   THE END OF THE PRIVATE LANDLORD   Fabian Society, 1973

Edwards, Q.   SHAW'S GUIDE TO RENT CONTROL AND THE INCREASE OF RENTS   Shaw, 1957

Evans, D.L.   LAW OF LANDLORD AND TENANT   Butterworth, 1974

Eversley, D.   RENTS AND SOCIAL POLICY   Fabian Society, 1955

Farrand, J.T.   THE RENT ACT, 1974   Sweet & Maxwell, 1975

Fawcett, W.M.   A CONCISE TREATISE ON THE LAW OF LANDLORD AND TENANT   (2nd ed by J.M. Lightwood)   Butterworths, 1900

Field-Fisher, T.G., Ibbotson, S. and Roydhouse, E. RENT REGULATION AND CONTROL Butterworth, 1967

Foa, E.C. GENERAL LAW OF LANDLORD AND TENANT (8th ed by H. Heathcote-Williams) Ipswich: Thames Bank Publishing, 1957

Gray, P.G. and Parr, E. RENT ACT, 1957, REPORT OF INQUIRY (Cmnd. 1246) HMSO, 1960

G.B. Committee of the Ministry of Reconstruction on the Increase of Rent and Mortgage Interest (War Restrictions) Act, 1915 REPORT (Cd. 9235) HMSO, 1918

G.B. Committee on Housing in Greater London REPORT (Chairman: Sir Milner Holland) (Cmnd. 2605) HMSO, 1965

G.B. Committee on the Alleged Recent Increases in the Rental of small Dwelling-houses in Industrial districts in Scotland REPORT (Cd. 8111) (Evidence, Appendices and Index, Cd. 8154) HMSO, 1916

G.B. Committee on the Increase of Rent and Mortgage Interest (War Restrictions) Acts REPORT (Cmd. 658) HMSO, 1920

G.B. Committee on the Rent Acts REPORT (Chairman: H.E. Francis) (Cmnd. 4609) HMSO, 1971

G.B. Committee on the Rent Restrictions Acts (Scotland) REPORT (Cmd. 2423) HMSO, 1923

G.B. Departmental Committee on the Increase of Rent and Mortgage Interest (Restrictions) Act, 1920 FINAL REPORT (Cmd. 1803) HMSO, 1923

G.B. Government POLICY ON RENT RESTRICTION (Cmd. 5667) HMSO, 1938

G.B. Home Department GOVERNMENT POLICY ON LEASEHOLD PROPERTY IN ENGLAND & WALES (Cmd. 8713) HMSO, 1953

G.B. Interdepartmental Committee REPORT (Cmd. 3911) HMSO, 1931

G.B. Interdepartmental Committee FURTHER REPORT (Cmd. 5621) HMSO, 1938

G.B. Interdepartmental Committee on Rent Control REPORT (Cmd. 6621) HMSO, 1945

G.B. Law Commission CODIFICATION OF THE LAW OF LANDLORD AND TENANT: REPORT ON OBLIGATIONS OF LANDLORDS AND TENANTS (Law Comm: No. 67) HMSO, 1975

G.B. Law Commission LANDLORD AND TENANT. INTERIM REPORT ON DISTRESS FOR RENT HMSO, 1966

G.B. Law Commission WORKING PAPER No. 25: PROPOSALS RELATING TO COVENANTS RESTRICTING DISPOSITIONS, PARTING WITH POSSESSION, CHANGE OF USER AND ALTERATIONS Law Commission, 1970

G.B. Ministry of Housing and Local Government RENT CONTROL: STATIS-TICAL INFORMATION (Cmnd. 17) HMSO, 1956

G.B. Ministry of Housing and Local Government   RENT ACT, 1957 REPORT
        OF INQUIRY (Cmnd. 1246) HMSO, 1960
G.B. Ministry of Housing and Local Government   RESIDENTIAL LEASE–
        HOLD PROPERTY (Cmnd. 1789) HMSO, 1962
G.B. Ministry of Land and Natural Resources   LEASEHOLD REFORM IN
        ENGLAND & WALES (Cmnd. 2916) HMSO, 1966
G.B. Parliament Select Committee on TOWN HOLDINGS   REPORT (H.C.251/
        1889) Hansard, 1889
G.B. Royal Commission on the HOUSING OF THE WORKING CLASS, C.4402
        and C. 4402–I HMSO, 1885
Greve, J. PRIVATE LANDLORDS IN ENGLAND Bell, 1965
Griffin, R.W.   SECURITY OF TENURE AND THE FIXING OF RENTS
        Shelter Housing Aid Centre, 1975
Hague, N.T. LEASEHOLD ENFRANCHISEMENT Sweet & Maxwell, 1967
Harvey, A. TENANTS IN DANGER Harmondsworth: Penguin, 1964
Hawkins, A.J. LAW RELATING TO OWNERS AND OCCUPIERS OF LAND
        Butterworths, 1971
Heddle, J. and Linacre, V. A NEW LEASE OF LIFE: A SOLUTION TO
        RENT CONTROL Conservative Political Centre, 1975
Howe, G. and Jones, C. HOUSES TO LET: THE FUTURE OF RENT
        CONTROL Conservative Political Centre, 1956
Hill, H.A. and Redman, J.W. LAW OF LANDLORD AND TENANT
        (l6th ed) Butterworths, 1976
Jackson, B. LANDLORD AND TENANT RELATIONS: A SELECTED
        BIBLIOGRAPHY Sacramento: California State Library, Law
        Library, 1970
Jacobs, S. THE RIGHT TO A DECENT HOUSE Routledge & Kegan Paul,
        1976
Karlslake, H.H. LEASEHOLD REFORM ACT, 1967 Rating and Valuation
        Association, 1967
Lamont, D.H.L. RESIDENTIAL TENANCIES (2nd ed) Toronto: Carswell,
        1973
Lansley, S. and Fiegenhen, G. HOUSING ALLOWANCES AND INEQUAL–
        ITY Fabian Society, 1973
Legal Action Group LAW IN A HOUSING CRISIS   LAG, 1975
Levi, J.H. and others MODEL RESIDENTIAL LANDLORD–TENANT
        CODE Chicago: American Bar Foundation, 1969
Lewis, J.R. and Holland, J.A. LANDLORD AND TENANT Sweet &
        Maxwell, 1968
Lipsky, M. RENT STRIKES IN NEW YORK CITY: PROTEST POLITICS
        AND THE POWER OF THE POOR (Thesis – Princeton, 1967)
        University Microfilms, Ann Arbour, Mich, 1969
MacColl, J. A PLAN FOR RENTED HOUSES Fabian Society, 1957

Macmillan, S.K. LAW OF LEASES Estates Gazette, 1970

Macrae, N. TO LET? Hobart Paper 2, Institute for Economic Affairs, 1960

Macrae, N. RENT CONTROLS OR HOUSES? Property Council, 1964

Magnus, S.W. THE RENT ACT, 1968 Butterworth, 1969

Magnus, S.W. LEASEHOLD PROPERTY (TEMPORARY PROVISIONS) ACT, 1951 Butterworth, 1951, Supplement, 1953

Megarry, R.E. THE RENT ACTS (10th ed) Stevens, 1967 (Volume 3, 1970)

Morgan, S.E. SHAW'S GUIDE TO RENT CONTROL (3rd ed) Shaw & Sons, 1966

Munby, D.L. THE RENT PROBLEM Fabian Society, 1952

Nelson-Jones, J. HOME TRUTHS Conservative Political Centre, 1966

New York University School of Law HOUSING FOR THE POOR: RIGHTS AND REMEDIES New York, 1967

Nevitt, A.A. HOUSING, TAXATION AND SUBSIDIES: A STUDY OF HOUSING IN THE UNITED KINGDOM Nelson, 1966

Ontario Law Reform Commission INTERIM REPORT ON LANDLORD AND TENANT LAW Toronto: Department of Attorney General, 1968

Page, D. and Weinberger, B. BIRMINGHAM RENT REBATE AND ALLOW— ANCE STUDY Birmingham: Centre for Urban and Regional Studies, 1975

Page, R.G. and Leaper, W.J. THE RENT ACT, 1965 Estates Gazette, 1966

Partington, M. LANDLORD AND TENANT Weidenfeld & Nicolson, 1975

Paton, G.C.H. and Cameron, J.G.S. LAW OF LANDLORD AND TENANT IN SCOTLAND Edinburgh: Green, 1967

Pearson, P. A NEW DEAL FOR FURNISHED TENANTS Shelter, 1973

Pennance, F.G. (ed) VERDICT ON RENT CONTROL Institute of Economic Affairs, 1972

Power, A. DAVID AND GOLIATH: BARNSBURY 1973 Holloway Neighbourhood Law Centre, 1973

Reid, R. THE RENT ACT, 1968, AS AMENDED BY THE HOUSING ACT 1969 Estates Gazette, 1969

Reid, R. THE RENT ACTS 1968 and 1974 Estates Gazette Ltd., 1976

Rose, J.G. LANDLORDS AND TENANTS New Brunswick, N.J; Transaction Books, 1973

Rossi, H. SHAW'S GUIDE TO THE RENT ACT, 1974 Shaw, 1974

Roydhouse, E. THE RENT ACT, 1965 Butterworth, 1965

Sackville, R. HOMELESS PEOPLE AND THE LAW Canberra: Australian Govt. Print Service, 1976

Seward, G. and Stewart-Smith, W.R. RENT ACT, 1965 Rating and Valuation Association, 1965

Seward, G. and Stewart-Smith, W.R. LEASEHOLD REFORM ACT Knight,

1968

Shelter NOTICE TO QUIT Shelter, 1968

Smith, H. A MANUAL OF THE LAW OF LANDLORD AND TENANT
  Davis & Son, 1871

Sternlieb, G. THE TENEMENT LANDLORD New Brunswick, N.J: Urban
  Studies Center, Rutgers State University, 1966

Tiplady, D. HOUSING WELFARE LAW Oyez Publishing, 1975

U.S. Department of Housing and Urban Development THE LANDLORD–
  TENANT RELATIONSHIP: A SELECTED BIBLIOGRAPHY
  Washington: U.S. Govt. Print Off., 1971

Wellings, V.G. AN OUTLINE OF THE LAW OF LANDLORD AND TENANT
  Sweet & Maxwell, 1961

Whitfield, A.H. AN INTRODUCTION TO THE LAW OF LEASES Estates
  Gazette, 1961

Woodfall, W. LAW OF LANDLORD AND TENANT (27th ed by L.A.
  Blundell and V.G. Wellings) Sweet & Maxwell, 1968

(d)   CO-OPERATIVE HOUSING

Clurman, D. and Hebard, E.L. CONDOMINIUMS AND COOPERATIVES
  New York: Wiley-Interscience, 1970

G.B. Central Housing Advisory Committee HOUSING ASSOCIATION
  HMSO, 1971

G.B. Department of the Environment HOUSING FINANCE ACT, 1972:
  MEMORANDUM ON HOUSING ASSOCIATIONS HMSO, 1972

G.B. Working Party on Housing Cooperatives FINAL REPORT HMSO, 1976

Goldstein, L. COMMUNES: LAW AND COMMON SENSE Boston, Mass:
  New Community Projects, 1974

P.E.P. HOUSING ASSOCIATIONS (Vol. XXVIII, No. 462, Planning)
  Political and Economic Planning, 1962

Rosenberg, A.B. CONDOMINIUM IN CANADA (looseleaf) Toronto:
  Canada Law Book, 1969

U.S. Department of Housing and Urban Development Library Information
  Division CONDOMINIUM AND COOPERATIVE HOUSING 1960-
  1971: BIBLIOGRAPHY Washington, D.C: U.S. Govt. Print Off.,
  1972

(e)   AGRICULTURAL TENANCIES: TIED ACCOMMODATION

G.B. DepartmentalCommittee on Position of Tenant Farmers on the Occasion
  of any change in the Ownership of their Holdings etc. REPORT

(Cd. 6030)   HMSO, 1912

G.B. Department of the Environment   ABOLITION OF THE TIED COTTAGE SYSTEM IN AGRICULTURE: CONSULTATIVE DOCUMENT Department of the Environment, 1975

G.B. Ministry of Agriculture, Fisheries and Food   AGRICULTURAL LAND, RIGHTS AND OBLIGATIONS OF LANDLORDS AND TENANTS (5th ed) HMSO, 1969

Irving, B.L. and Hilgendorf, E.L.   TIED COTTAGES IN BRITISH AGRI-CULTURE; WORKING PAPER NO. 1 – BASIC STATISTICS Tavistock Institute for Human Relationships, 1975

Jones, A.   RURAL HOUSING: THE AGRICULTURAL TIED COTTAGE (Occasional Paper on Social Administration No. 56) Geo. Bell & Sons, 1975

Muir Watt   AGRICULTURAL HOLDINGS (12th ed)   Sweet & Maxwell, 1967

Mustoe, N.E.   AGRICULTURAL LAW AND TENANT RIGHT (5th ed) Estates Gazette, 1959

Orwin, C.S. and Peel, W.R.   THE TENURE OF AGRICULTURAL LAND Cambridge University Press, 1925

Scammell, W.S.   LAW OF AGRICULTURAL HOLDINGS (4th ed) Butterworth, 1964

Walsmley, R.C.   AGRICULTURAL ARBITRATIONS   Estates Gazette, 1970

Ward, J.T.   FARM RENTS AND TENURE   Estates Gazette, 1959

(f)   HOUSING CONDITIONS, URBAN RENEWAL AND
                          PUBLIC HEALTH

Barnes, H.   HOUSING, THE FACTS AND THE FUTURE   Benn, 1923

Barnes, H.   THE SLUM, ITS STORY AND SOLUTION   P.S. King & Son, 1931

Beattie, D.J.   THE PUBLIC HEALTH ACT, 1936   Solicitors Law Stationery Society Ltd., 1937

Bigham, D.A.   LAW AND ADMINISTRATION RELATING TO PROTECTION OF THE ENVIRONMENT   Oyez Publishing, 1973

Blitz, L.F.   URBAN RENEWAL: ITS IMPACT ON MUNICIPAL ADMINI-STRATION   Ann Arbour, Mich: University Microfilms, 1967

Bramall, A.   A GUIDE TO THE HOUSING REPAIRS AND RENTS ACT, 1954 (2nd ed)   Sweet & Maxwell, 1954

Centre for Urban and Regional Studies   BEECHES ROAD AREA STUDY: A POTENTIAL HOUSING ACTION AREA   University of Birmingham, 1975

Clarke, J.J.   THE LAW OF HOUSING AND PLANNING, including PUBLIC

HEALTH, HIGHWAYS AND THE ACQUISITION OF LAND (3rd ed)
Pitman, 1936
Community Action HOW TO FIGHT FOR BETTER HOUSING CONDITIONS
Community Action, 1973
Community Development Project THE POVERTY OF THE IMPROVEMENT
PROGRAMME CDP Information and Intelligence Unit, 1975
Davies, F.G. and Whiteside, J. PUBLIC HEALTH PRECEDENTS
Knight, 1966
Davies, K. WEST'S LAW OF HOUSING The Estates Gazette, 1974
Ferguson, T. and others PUBLIC HEALTH AND URBAN GROWTH Centre
for Urban Studies, University College, 1964
Fletcher, B. DILAPIDATONS (6th ed) Batsford, 1966
Friedman, L.M. GOVERNMENT AND SLUM HOUSING, A CENTURY OF
FRUSTRATION Chicago: Rand McNally, 1968
Garner, J.F. SLUM CLEARANCE AND COMPENSATION (2nd ed) Oyez
Publications, 1970
Grad, F.P. LEGAL REMEDIES FOR HOUSING CODE VIOLATIONS
Washington: U.S. Govt. Print Off., 1968
Glasgow Planning Department THE SPRINGBURN STUDY: URBAN RE—
NEWAL IN A REGIONAL CONTEXT Glasgow: City Council
Planning Department, 1967
G.B. Central Housing Advisory Committee HOMES FOR TODAY AND TO—
MORROW (Chairman: Parker Morris) HMSO, 1961
G.B. Central Housing Advisory Committee OUR OLDER HOMES: A CALL
FOR ACTON (Chairman: E. Denington) HMSO, 1966
G.B. Law Commission CODIFICATION OF LAW OF LANDLORD AND
TENANT: REPORT ON OBLIGATIONS OF LANDLORDS AND
TENANTS (H.C. 377/1974-75) HMSO, 1975
G.B. Ministry of Housing and Local Government OLD HOUSES INTO NEW
HOMES HMSO, 1968
Greater London Council THE CONDITION OF LONDON'S HOUSING – A
SURVEY G.L.C., 1970
Gregory, P. POLLUTED HOMES (Occasional Papers on Social Administration
No. 15) Bell, 1965
Hart, T. THE COMPREHENSIVE DEVELOPMENT AREA Edinburgh:
Oliver & Boyd, 1968
Hill, H.A. THE COMPLETE LAW OF HOUSING (4th ed) Butterworth,
1947 (2nd supplement, 1951)
Hunter, D.V. THE SLUMS: CHALLENGE AND RESPONSE New York:
Free Press, 1968
Kerse, C.S. NOISE Oyez Publishing, 1975
Lawson, M.B.M. THE MAINTENANCE OF PROPERTY: A PROGAM FOR
ONTARIO (Report to Department of Municipal Affairs) Toronto:

1970

Local Government Library   ENCYCLOPAEDIA OF HOUSING LAW AND
    PRACTICE   Sweet & Maxwell, 1958 (updated by looseleaf service)

Local Government Library   ENCYCLOPAEDIA OF PUBLIC HEALTH LAW
    AND PRACTICE   Sweet & Maxwell, 1968 (update by looseleaf
    service)

Lumley's PUBLIC HEALTH (12th ed by E. Simes K.D. and C.E. Scholfield,
    Butterworths, 1959, 14 vols. 1974 and Fifth Cumulative Supplement,
    1974

Macey, J. HOUSING ACT 1974   Butterworths, 1975

Magnus, S.W. and Price, F.E.   Knight's ANNOTATED HOUSING ACT
    Knight, 1968

Millward, S. (ed) URBAN RENEWAL, 1967 (Symposium papers) Salford,
    University of Salford, Department of Civil Engineering, 1967

Muchnick, D.M. URBAN RENEWAL IN LIVERPOOL   Bell, 1970

McLouglin, J. THE LAW RELATING TO POLLUTION: AN
    INTRODUCTION   Manchester University Press, 1972

Noise Abatment Society   LAW ON NOISE   Noise Abatement Society, 1969

Pearson, P. and Henney, A. HOME IMPROVEMENT – PEOPLE OR
    PROFIT? Shelter, 1972

Quigley, H. and Goldie, I. HOUSING AND SLUM CLEARANCE IN
    LONDON Methuen, 1934

Roddis, R.J. THE HOUSING ACT, 1964 Butterworths, 1965

Schofield, A.N. HOUSING LAW AND PRACTICE (4th ed by A.N. Schofield
    and H.B. Sales) 2 vols.   Shaw, 1966

Shelter CONDEMNED Shelter, 1971

Simon, Sir E.D. THE ANTI-SLUM CAMPAIGN Longmans, Green, 1933

Tovell, L. (ed) HOUSING ACT 1961 Knight, 1962

U.S. Department of Housing and Urban Development   NEIGHBORHOOD
    CONSERVATION AND PROPERTY REHABILITATION (Biblio-
    graphy) Washington, 1969

U.S. Federal Housing Administration   REHABILITATION GUIDE FOR
    RESIDENTIAL PROPERTIES Washington, D.C: U.S. Govt. Print
    Off., 1968

West, W.A. THE LAW OF DILAPIDATIONS, WITH SOME HINTS ON
    PRACTICE (7th ed) Estates Gazette, 1974

West, W.A. LAW OF HOUSING (3rd ed by K. Davies) Estates Gazette,
    1974

Wilson, G. THE HOUSING ACT 1961 Butterworths, 1962

Wilson, J.Q. URBAN RENEWAL: THE RECORD AND THE CONTRO–
    VERSY Cambridge, Mass: M.I.T. Press, 1966

Vereker, C. and Mays, J.B. URBAN REDEVELOPMENT AND SOCIAL
    CHANGE Liverpool: University Press, 1961

Blundell and Dobry's PLANNING APPEALS AND INQUIRIES by Rose, P.L. and Barnes, M. (2nd ed) Sweet & Maxwell, 1970

Blundell, L.A. and Dobry, G. TOWN AND COUNTRY PLANNING Sweet & Maxwell, 1963

Broady, M. PLANNING FOR PEOPLE: ESSAYS ON THE SOCIAL CONTEXT OF PLANNING National Council of Social Science, 1968

Brown, H.J.J. PLANNING APPEALS Sweet & Maxwell, 1951

Brown, H.J.J. PRACTICAL POINTS ON PLANNING LAW Sweet & Maxwell, 1951

Charlesworth, J. THE PRINCIPLES OF PLANNING LAW (2nd ed) Stevens, 1948

Cherry, G. TOWN PLANNING IN ITS SOCIAL CONTEXT Leonard Hill, 1970

Clarke, J.J. LAW OF HOUSING AND PLANNING Pitman & Sons, 1936

Cowan, P. and Donnison, D.V. THE FUTURE OF PLANNING Heinemann, 1973

Cullingworth, J.B. and Orr, S.C. REGIONAL AND URBAN STUDIES: A SOCIAL SCIENCE APPROACH Allan & Unwin, c. 1969

Cullingworth, J.B. TOWN AND COUNTRY PLANNING IN ENGLAND AND WALES (3rd ed) Allen & Unwin, 1971

Davies, M.R.R. PRINCIPLES AND PRACTICE OF PLANNING Butter-worth, 1956

Dennis, N. PEOPLE AND PLANNING: THE SOCIOLOGY OF HOUSING IN SUNDERLAND Faber, 1970

Dennis, N. PUBLIC PARTICIPATION AND PLANNERS' BLIGHT Faber, 1972

Dobry, G. REVIEW OF THE DEVELOPMENT CONTROL SYSTEM Interim Report HMSO, 1974

Elkin, S.L. POLITICS AND LAND USE PLANNING Cambridge University Press, 1974

Frank, D. ENFORCEMENT OF PLANNING CONTROL UNDER THE TOWN AND COUNTRY PLANNING ACT, 1947 Estates Gazette, 1958

Friend, J.K. and Jessop, W.N. LOCAL GOVERNMENT AND STRATEGIC CHOICE Tavistock, 1969

Garner, J.F. PLANNING LAW IN WESTERN EUROPE Amsterdam: North-Holland, 1975

G.B. Committee on Public Participation in Planning PEOPLE AND PLANNING: A REPORT HMSO, 1969

G.B. Ministry of Housing and Local Government SELECTED PLANNING APPEALS HMSO, 1959-1963

G.B. Ministry of Housing and Local Government   TOWN AND COUNTRY
PLANNING (Cmnd. 3333)   HMSO, 1967

G.B. Preservation Policy Group   REPORT TO MINISTER OF HOUSING AND
LOCAL GOVERNMENT   HMSO, 1970

Haar, C.M.   LAND PLANNING LAW IN A FREE SOCIETY   Cambridge:
Harvard University Press, 1951

Haar, C.M. (ed)   LAW AND LAND: ANGLO-AMERICAN PLANNING
PRACTICE   Cambridge, Mass: Harvard University Press, 1964

Hagman, D.C.   PUBLIC PLANNING AND CONTROL OF URBAN AND
LAND DEVELOPMENT: CASES AND MATERIALS   St. Paul,
Minn: West Pub. Co., 1973

Hamilton, R.N.D.   A GUIDE TO DEVELOPMENT AND PLANNING (6th ed)
Oyez Publishing, 1975

Heap, D.   ENCYCLOPAEDIA OF PLANNING: LAW AND PRACTICE
Sweet & Maxwell, 1959

Heap, Sir D.   THE LAND AND THE DEVELOPMENT: OR THE TURMOIL
AND THE TORMENT   Sweet & Maxwell, 1975

Heap, D.   AN OUTLINE OF PLANNING LAW (6th ed) Sweet & Maxwell,
1973

Heap, D.   PLANNING LAW FOR TOWN AND COUNTRY   Sweet & Maxwell,
1938

Howard, E.   GARDEN CITIES OF TOMORROW   Faber, 1962

Keeble, L.   TOWN PLANNING AT THE CROSSROADS   Estates Gazette,
1961

Lamb, P. and Evans, M.   LAW AND PRACTICE OF TOWN AND COUNTRY
PLANNING   Staples Press, 1951

Little, A.J.   THE ENFORCEMENT OF PLANNING CONTROL (3rd ed)
Shaw & Sons, 1972

McAuslan, P.   LAND, LAW AND PLANNING   Weidenfeld & Nicolson, 1975

McCullock, F.J. and others   LAND USE IN AN URBAN ENVIRONMENT
Liverpool: University Press, 1961

McKown, R.   COMPREHENSIVE GUIDE TO TOWN PLANNING LAW AND
PROCEDURES (2nd ed) Godwin, 1974

McLoughlin, J.B.   URBAN AND REGIONAL PLANNING   New York:
Praeger, 1969

McLoughlin, J.B.   CONTROL AND URBAN PLANNING   Faber, 1973

Mandelker, D.R.   GREEN BELTS AND URBAN GROWTH   Madison: University of Wisconsin Press, 1962

Mandelker, D.R.   MANAGING OUR URBAN ENVIRONMENT (2nd ed)
Indianapolis: Bobbs-Merrill, 1971

Pooley, B.J.   THE EVOLUTION OF BRITISH PLANNING LEGISLATION
Ann Arbor: University of Michigan Law School, 1960

Roberts, N.A.   THE REFORM OF PLANNING LAW   Macmillan, 1976

Rose, R. (ed) THE MANAGEMENT OF URBAN CHANGE IN BRITAIN AND GERMANY   London and Beverley Hills: Sage Publicatons, 1974

Sagalyn, L.B. and Sternlieb, G.   ZONING AND HOUSING COSTS   Rutgers University, N.J: Center for Urban Policy and Research, 1973

Stewart, C.   A PROSPECT OF CITIES   Longmans, Green, 1952

Taylor, V.M.   STATUTORY INTERVENTION IN PRIVATE LAND USE CONTROL   College of Estate Management, 1966

Telling, A.E.   PLANNING LAW AND PROCEDURE   (5th ed)   Butterworths, 1976

West, W.A., Pennance, F.G. and Scammell, E.H.   THE PRIVATE CONTROL OF LAND USE   (Occasional Papers in Estate Management No. 1) College of Estate Management, 1966

Wood, Sir K.   THE LAW AND PRACTICE WITH REGARD TO HOUSING IN ENGLAND AND WALES   Hodder & Stoughton, 1921

(h)   COMPULSORY PURCHASE

Anon.   COMPENSATION FOR COMPULSORY PURCHASE   (Conference Papers) Sweet & Maxwell, 1975

Boynton, J.K.   COMPULSORY PURCHASE AND COMPENSATION   (3rd ed) Oyez Publishing, 1974

Brown, H.J.J.   ENCYCLOPAEDIA OF COMPULSORY PURCHASE AND COMPENSATION   Sweet & Maxwell, 1960

Corfield, F.V.   COMPENSATON AND THE TOWN AND COUNTRY PLANNING ACT, 1959   Solicitor's Law Stationery Society, 1959

Cripps, C.A.   COMPULSORY ACQUISITION   (11th ed plus supplements) Stevens, 1962

Davies, K.   LAW OF COMPULSORY PURCHASE AND COMPENSATION (2nd ed) Butterworths, 1975

Garner, J.F.   SLUM CLEARANCE AND COMPENSATION   (4th ed)   Oyez Publications, 1975

G.B. Department of the Environment   DEVELOPMENT AND COMPENSA–TION – PUTTING PEOPLE FIRST (Cmnd. 5124) HMSO, 1972

G.B. Expert Committee on Compensation and Betterment   FINAL REPORT (Cmd. 6386) HMSO, 1942

Justice   COMPENSATION FOR COMPULSORY ACQUISITION AND REMEDIES FOR PLANNING RESTRICTION   Stevens, 1969 (with supplemental report, 1973)

Lawrence, D.M.   COMPULSORY PURCHASE AND COMPENSATION (5th ed) Estates Gazette, 1972

Leach, W.A.   DISTURBANCE ON COMPULSORY PURCHASE   (2nd ed)

Estates Gazette, 1965

Nicholls, A.W. COMPENSATION FOR THE COMPULSORY ACQUISITION
OF LAND Hadleigh: Thames Bank, 1952

Nutley, W.G. and Beaumont, C.H. LAND COMPENSATION ACT, 1973
Butterworths, 1974

Stewart-Brown, R. A GUIDE TO COMPULSORY PURCHASE AND
COMPENSATION (5th ed) Sweet & Maxwell, 1962

(i)　　PUBLIC PARTICIPATION

Alinsky, S.D. REVEILLE FOR RADICALS New York: Vintage Books,
1969

Alinsky, S.D. RULES FOR RADICALS New York: Random House, 1971

Fabian Society PEOPLE, PARTICIPATION AND GOVERNMENT Fabian
Research Series 293   Fabian Society, 1971

Ledyard, J. (compiler) CITIZEN PARTICIPATION IN PLANNING (Bibliography) Monticello, Illinois: Council of Planning Librarians, 1969

Linowes, R.R. and D.T. Allensworth THE POLITICS OF LAND USE New
York: Praeger, c.1973

Marris, P. and Rein, P. DILEMMAS OF SOCIAL REFORM: POVERTY
AND COMMUNITY ACTION IN THE U.S. Harmondsworth:
Penguin, 1973

Milbrath, L.W. POLITICAL PARTICIPATION Chicago, Ill: Rand McNally,
1965

Rees, L.B. GOVERNMENT BY COMMUNITY Knight, 1971

Scheingold, Stuart A. THE POLITICS OF RIGHTS: LAWYERS, PUBLIC
POLICY AND POLITICAL CHANGE New Haven: Yale University
Press, 1974

Skeffington, A. PEOPLE AND PLANNING   HMSO, 1969

U.S. Department of Housing and Urban Development CITIZEN AND
BUSINESS PARTICIPATION IN URBAN AFFAIRS; A BIBLIO—
GRAPHY Washington, D.C: U.S. Govt. Print Off., 1970

Birks, M. SMALL CLAIMS IN THE COUNTY COURT   Lord Chancellor's Office, 1973

Borrie, G. and Diamond, A.L. THE CONSUMER, SOCIETY AND THE LAW (3rd ed) Harmondsworth: Penguin, 1973

Caplovitz, D. CONSUMERS IN TROUBLE New York: Free Press, 1974

Consumer Council CONSUMER CONSULTATIVE MACHINERY IN THE NATIONALISED INDUSTRIES   HMSO, 1968

Consumer Council JUSTICE OUT OF REACH   HMSO, 1970

Consumer Council REPORTS (1963/64 – 1969/70) HMSO, annual

Crown, P. LEGAL PROTECTION FOR THE CONSUMER Dobbs Ferry, New York: Oceana Publications, 1963

Cunningham, J.P. THE FAIR TRADING ACT 1973: CONSUMER PROTEC-TION AND COMPETITION LAW Sweet & Maxwell, 1974

Curran, B.A. TRENDS IN CONSUMER CREDIT LEGISLATION Chicago: University of Chicago Press, 1965

Elbrecht, R.A. CONSUMER LAW BIBLIOGRAPHY Brighton, Mass: National Consumer Law Center, Boston College Law School, 1971

Forman, P. THE TRADE DESCRIPTIONS ACT, 1968: A LAWYER'S PROGRESS REPORT Consumer Council, 1970

Fox-Smith, V.R. HIRE PURCHASE, CREDIT AND FINANCE Stevens, 1962

Giordan, M. THE CONSUMER JUNGLE Fontana, 1974

G.B. Committee on Consumer Credit REPORT (Chairman: Lord Crowther) (Cmnd. 4596) HMSO, 1971

G.B. Committee on Consumer Protection FINAL REPORT (Chairman: J.T. Moloney) (Cmnd. 1781) HMSO, 1962

G.B. Committee on the Enforcement of Judgment Debts REPORT (Chairman: The Hon. Mr. Justice Payne) (Cmnd. 3909) HMSO, 1969

G.B. Department of Trade and Industry REFORM OF THE LAW ON CONSUMER CREDIT (Cmnd. 5427) HMSO, 1973

G.B. Departmental Committee on Imprisonment by Courts of Summary Jurisdiction in Default of Payment of Fines and Other Sums of Money (Cmd. 4649) HMSO, 1934

G.B. Office of Fair Trading A REVIEW OF THE TRADE DESCRIPTIONS ACT: CONSULTATIVE DOCUMENT Office of Fair Trading, 1975

Goode, R.M. CONSUMER CREDIT ACT, 1974 Butterworths, 1974

Havenger, J.J.D. RETAILING: COMPETITION AND TRADE PRACTICES Leiden, A.W. Sijthoff, 1973

Howe, Sir G. ACTION FOR THE CONSUMER Conservative Political Centre, 1973

Hunter, A. COMPETITION AND THE LAW Allen & Unwin, 1966

Katz, C.H. THE LAW AND THE LOW INCOME CONSUMER New York,
New York: University School of Law, 1968

Kelly, D. St. L. DEBT RECOVERY IN AUSTRALIA Canberra: Australian
Govt. Print Serv., 1976

Korah, V. MONOPOLIES AND RESTRICTIVE PRACTICES Harmondsworth: Penguin, 1968

Leaper, W.J. IMPLICATIONS FOR BUSINESS OF THE NEW TRADE
DESCRIPTIONS LAW Business Books Ltd., 1968

Liberal Party THE CONSUMER'S CHARTER (Report of the Consumer
Affairs Panel) Liberal Publication Department, 1968

Martin, J. and Smith, G.W. THE CONSUMER INTEREST Pall Mall, 1968

Mayo, O.G. (ed) CONSUMER CREDIT CONTROL Gower Press, 1971

NOP Market Research Ltd. SURVEYS ON CONSUMER CREDIT Department of Trade and Industry, 1971

O'Keefe, J.A. THE LAW RELATING TO TRADE DESCRIPTIONS (looseleaf)
Butterworths, 1971

Ontario Legislative Assembly Select Committee on Consumer Credit FINAL
REPORT (Sessional Paper No. 85, 1965) Toronto, 1965

Pickering, J.F. RESALE PRICE MAINTENANCE IN PRACTICE Allen &
Unwin, 1966

Rock, P. MAKING PEOPLE PAY Routledge & Kegan Paul, 1973

Rothschild, D.P. and Carroll, D.W. CONSUMER PROTECTION Cincinatti:
W.H. Anderson, 1973

Rudinger, E. (ed) HOW TO SUE IN THE COUNTY COURT Consumers'
Association, 1974

Solomon, G.L. THE RADICAL CONSUMER'S HANDBOOK New York:
Ballantine Books, 1972

Stevens, R.B. and Yamey, B.S. THE RESTRICTIVE PRACTICES COURT
Weidenfeld & Nicolson, 1965

Tench, D. THE LAW FOR CONSUMERS (Rev. ed. by Edith Rudinger)
Consumers Association, 1970

Titchiner, L. and Winyard, A. CONSUMERS' RIGHTS Arrow, 1975

U.S. Office of Economic Affairs CONSUMER EDUCATION BIBLIOGRAPHY
Washington: U.S. Govt. Print Off., 1971

Whincup, M.H. CONSUMER PROTECTION LAW IN AMERICA, CANADA
AND EUROPE (National Prices Commission Occasional Paper No. 9)
Dublin: Stationery Office, 1973

VI   THE CITIZEN AND THE STATE

(a)   GENERAL ADMINISTRATIVE LAW

Allen, Sir C.K. BUREAUCRACY TRIUMPHANT Oxford University Press, 1931

Allen, Sir C.K. ADMINISTRATIVE JURISDICTION Stevens, 1956

Allen, Sir C.K. LAW AND ORDER: AN INQUIRY INTO THE NATURE AND SCOPE OF DELEGATED LEGISLATION AND EXECUTIVE POWERS IN ENGLISH LAW Stevens, 1965

Australia: Commonwealth Administrative Review Committee REPORT (Parliamentary Paper No. 144, 1971) Canberra: Commonwealth Govt. Print Off., 1971

Borrie, G. PUBLIC LAW Sweet & Maxwell, 1970

Buxton, R. LOCAL GOVERNMENT (2nd ed) Harmondsworth: Penguin, 1973

Carr, Sir C.T. CONCERNING ENGLISH ADMINISTRATIVE LAW New York: Columbia University Press, 1941

Cross, C.A. THE LOCAL GOVERNMENT ACT, 1972 Sweet & Maxwell, 1973

Cross, C.A. PRINCIPLES OF LOCAL GOVERNMENT LAW (5th ed) Sweet & Maxwell, 1974

Davis, K.C. ADMINISTRATIVE JUSTICE (2nd ed) St. Paul's, Minnesota: West Publishing Co.

de Smith, S.A. CONSTITUTIONAL AND ADMINISTRATIVE LAW (2nd ed) Harmondsworth: Penguin, 1973

de Smith, S.A. JUDICIAL REVIEW OF ADMINISTRATIVE ACTION (3rd ed) Stevens, 1973

Dicey, A.V. LAW OF THE CONSTITUTION (10th ed) Macmillan, 1959

Elcock, H.J. ADMINISTRATIVE JUSTICE Longmans, 1969

Foulkes, D. INTRODUCTION TO ADMINISTRATIVE LAW (3rd ed) Butterworth, 1972

Garner, J.F. ADMINISTRATIVE LAW (4th ed) Butterworths, 1974

Ganz, G. ADMINISTRATIVE PROCEDURES Sweet & Maxwell, 1974

G.B. Committee on Administrative Tribunals and Enquiries REPORT (Chairman: Sir O. Franks) (Cmnd. 218) HMSO, 1957

G.B. Committee on Ministers' Powers REPORT (Chairman: Lord Donoughmore) (Cmd. 4060) HMSO, 1932

G.B. Law Commission (Working Paper No. 40) REMEDIES IN ADMINISTRATIVE LAW HMSO, 1971

G.B. Law Commission ADMINISTRATIVE LAW (Cmnd. 4059) HMSO, 1969.

G.B. Law Commission REMEDIES IN ADMINISTRATIVE LAW (Report No.
        73) HMSO, 1976

Griffith, J.A.G. and Street, H. PRINCIPLES OF ADMINISTRATIVE LAW
        (5th ed) Pitman, 1973

Hamson, C.J. EXECUTIVE DISCRETION AND JUDICIAL CONTROL
        Stevens, 1954

Hart, W.O. and Garner, J.F. HART'S LOCAL GOVERNMENT AND
        ADMINISTRATION (9th ed) Butterworths, 1973

Hewart, Lord L., C.J. THE NEW DESPOTISM Benn, 1929

Hill, M.T. THE SOCIOLOGY OF PUBLIC ADMINISTRATION Weidenfeld
        & Nicolson, 1972

Inns of Court Conservative & Unionist Society RULE OF LAW Conser-
        vative Political Centre, 1955

Inns of Court Conservative & Unionist Society LET RIGHT BE DONE
        Conservative Political Centre, 1966

Jaffe, L.L. JUDICIAL CONTROL OF ADMINISTRATIVE ACTION Boston:
        Little, Brown, 1965

Jennings, Sir I. PRINCIPLES OF LOCAL GOVERNMENT LAW (4th ed.
        by J.A.G. Griffith) University of London Press, 1960

Jowell, J.L. LAW AND BUREAUCRACY Port Washington, New York:
        Dunellen Publishing Co., 1975

Justice THE CITIZEN AND THE ADMINISTRATION (Whyatt Report)
        Stevens, 1961

Justice ADMINISTRATION UNDER THE LAW Stevens, 1971

Lawson, F.H. REMEDIES OF ENGLISH LAW Harmondsworth: Penguin,
        1972

Lawson, F.H. and Bentley, D.J. CONSTITUTIONAL AND ADMINI–
        STRATIVE LAW Butterworths, 1961

Nonet, P. ADMINISTRATIVE JUSTICE: ADVOCACY AND CHANGE IN
        A GOVERNMENT AGENCY New York, Russell Sage Foundation, 19

Phillips, O.H. CONSTITUTIONAL AND ADMINISTRATIVE LAW (5th ed)
        Sweet & Maxwell, 1970

Robinson, G.E. PUBLIC AUTHORITIES AND LEGAL LIABILITY London
        University Press, 1925

Robson, W.A. JUSTICE AND ADMINISTRATIVE LAW (3rd ed) Stevens,
        1951

Samuels, H. APPEALS FROM THE DECISIONS OF LOCAL AUTHORITIES
        Solicitors' Law Stationery Society, 1935

Schwartz, B. and Wade, H.W.R. LEGAL CONTROL OF GOVERNMENT
        Oxford: Clarendon Press, 1972

Society of Conservative Lawyers YOUR RIGHTS; YOUR COURTS; YOUR
        INQUIRIES Society of Conservative Lawyers, 1970

Society of Conservative Lawyers ADMINISTRATIVE LAW – PROPOSALS

FOR AN ADMINISTRATIVE COURT   Conservative Political Centre,
1970
Street, H. GOVERNMENTAL LIABILITY   Cambridge: University Press,
1953
Street, H. JUSTICE IN THE WELFARE STATE (2nd ed)   Stevens, 1975
Wade, H.W.R. ADMINISTRATIVE LAW (3rd ed) Oxford: University Press,
1971
Wade, H.W.R. TOWARDS ADMINISTRATIVE JUSTICE   Oxford: University
Press, 1963
Williams, G. CROWN PROCEEDINGS   Stevens, 1948
Yardley, D.C.M. A SOURCE BOOK OF ADMINISTRATIVE LAW (2nd ed)
Butterworths, 1970
Zamir, I. THE DECLARATORY JUDGMENT   Stevens, 1962

(b)   TRIBUNALS AND INQUIRIES

Bell, K. TRIBUNALS IN THE SOCIAL SERVICES   Routledge & Kegan Paul,
1969
Council on Tribunals ANNUAL REPORTS   HMSO, 1959-date
Farmer, J.A. TRIBUNALS AND GOVERNMENT   Weidenfeld & Nicolson,
1974
Fulbrook, J., Brooke, R. and Archer, P. TRIBUNALS: A SOCIAL COURT?
Fabian Tract No. 427, 1973
Franks, Sir O. (Chairman) COMMITTEE ON ADMINISTRATIVE TRIBUNALS
AND ENQUIRIES (Cmnd. 218) HMSO, 1957
Herman, M. ADMINISTRATIVE JUSTICE AND SUPPLEMENTARY
BENEFITS Bell, 1972
Institutie of Judicial Administration   THE FUTURE OF ADMINISTRATIVE
TRIBUNALS University of Birmingham, 1971
Keeton, G.W. TRIAL BY TRIBUNAL Museum Press, 1960
Keith, K.J. A CODE OF PROCEDURE FOR ADMINISTRATIVE TRIBUNALS
Auckland, N.Z: Legal Research Foundation, School of Law, 1974
Pollard, R.S.W. (ed) ADMINISTRATIVE TRIBUNALS AT WORK Stevens,
1960
Vandyk, N.D.   TRIBUNALS & INQUIRIES: A GUIDE TO PROCEDURE
Oyez Publications, 1965
Wraith, R.E. and Hutchesson, P.G. ADMINISTRATIVE TRIBUNALS Allen
& Unwin, 1973
Wraith, R.E. and Lamb, G.B. PUBLIC INQUIRIES AS AN INSTRUMENT
OF GOVERNMENT Allen & Unwin, 1971

(c) OMBUDSMEN

Aaron, T.J. THE CONTROL OF POLICE DISCRETION: THE DANISH
    EXPERIENCE Springfield, Ill: Thomas, 1966
Anderson, S.V. OMBUDSMAN PAPERS Berkeley: Insititute of Governmental
    Studies, University of California, 1969
Gellhorn, W. OMBUDSMEN AND OTHERS: CITIZENS' PROTECTORS IN
    NINE COUNTRIES Harvard: University Press, 1966
G.B. Parliarmentary Commissioner for Administration REPORTS   HMSO,
    1967-date
G.B. Select Committee on the Parliamentary Commissioner for Administration
    REPORTS   HMSO, 1967-date
Gregory, R. and Hutchesson, P. THE PARLIAMENTARY OMBUDSMAN:
    A STUDY IN THE CONTROL OF ADMINISTRATIVE ACTION
    Allen & Unwin, 1975
Hiden, M. THE OMBUDSMAN IN FINLAND Berkeley: Institute of Govern-
    mental Studies, University of California, 1973
Hill, L.B. PARLIAMENT AND THE OMBUDSMAN IN NEW ZEALAND
    Norman: Bureau of Government Research, University of Oklahoma,
    1974
Justice THE CITIZEN AND THE ADMINISTRATION: THE REDRESS OF
    GRIEVANCES (Chairman: Sir John Wyatt) Stevens, 1961
Justice THE CITIZEN AND HIS COUNCIL: OMBUDSMEN FOR LOCAL
    GOVERNMENT (Chairman: J.F. Garner) Stevens, 1969
Keith-Lucas, B. and Arnold-Baker, C. AN OMBUDSMAN FOR LOCAL
    GOVERNMENT National Association of Parish Councils, 1969
Northern Ireland, Parliamentary Commissioner for Administration ANNUAL
    REPORTS   HMSO, Belfast, 1969-date
Peel, R.V. (ed) THE OMBUDSMAN OR CITIZEN'S DEFENDER (Special
    number of Annals of the American Academy of Political and Social
    Science) Philadelphia: A.A.P.S.S., 1968
Public Law, Special Number on the Idea of Ombudsman Stevens, 1962
Rowat, D.C. (ed) OMBUDSMAN: CITIZENS' DEFENDER (2nd ed) Allen
    & Unwin, 1968
Rowat, D.C. THE OMBUDSMAN PLAN Toronto: McClelland & Stewart,
    1973
Sawer, G. OMBUDSMEN (2nd ed) Cambridge University Press, 1968
South Carolina Department of Corrections INMATE GRIEVANCE PRO—
    CEDURES Columbia, 1973
Stacey, F. THE BRITISH OMBUDSMAN Oxford: Clarendon Press, 1971
Utley, T.E. OCCASION FOR OMBUDSMAN Johnson, 1961
Weeks, K.M. OMBUDSMEN AROUND THE WORLD Berkeley: Institute
    of Governmental Studies, University of California, 1973

Wheare, K.C. MALADMINISTRATION AND ITS REMEDIES Stevens, 1973

Wyner, A.J. (ed) EXECUTIVE OMBUDSMEN IN THE U.S. Berkeley:
    Institute of Governmental Studies, University of California, 1969

Wyner, A.J. THE NEBRASKA OMBUDSMAN: INNOVATION IN STATE
    GOVERNMENT Berkeley, California: Institute of Governmental
    Studies, University of California, 1974

FRANCES PINTER BOOKS

bibliographies

Modern British Society
John Westergaard, Anne Weyman, Paul Wiles
£2.50 *paperback*   £7.00 *hardback*

Social Policy and Administration in Britain
Tessa Blackstone
£1.50 *paperback*   £6.00 *hardback*

International Relations
A.J.R. Groom, Christopher Mitchell
£2.50 *paperback*   £7.00 *hardback*

Sociology of Education
Olive Banks
£7.00 *hardback*

monographs

Contemporary Social Mobility
C.J. Richardson
£7.00 *hardback*

Comprehensive Education and The Egalitarian Dream
J. Welton
£7.00 *hardback*

Adult Students: Education Selection and Social Control
Earl Hopper, Marilyn Osborn
£2.50 *paperback*   £6.00 *hardback*

Frances Pinter (Publishers) Ltd
161 West End Lane · London · NW6 2LG